Worker Mobility and Urban Policy in Latin America

This book argues that urban outcomes are better understood as the result of the interactions between policies from distinct policy domains rather than from any single policy silo. In doing so, this book develops and applies the Policy Interactions Framework to the study of the mobility experience of workers in Greater Mexico City.

Four empirical studies provide the reader with a comprehensive view of how urban policies can sometimes interact at cross-purposes to produce inequitable urban outcomes. The chapters analyze time and distance in the journey to work to quantify and map commuting inequalities, assess the shift in the spatial location of the demand for labor between 1999 and 2019, examine the default housing pathways available for workers, and evaluate the spatial distribution of public and common mobility resources. An outcome of applying the Policy Interactions Framework to the study of workers' mobility is to put forward the choiceless mobility hypothesis: a process by which the interaction between the spatial location of the demand for labor, the housing pathways available for workers, and the political economy of public transport operates to produce geographies of low accessibility to jobs.

The audience of this book consists of scholars and practitioners in the field of urban policy analysis, urban development, and urban political economy in the Global South.

David López-García is postdoctoral research associate in the Department of Urban Planning and Policy in the University of Illinois at Chicago, IL, USA.

Routledge Advances in Regional Economics, Science and Policy

Managing Knowledge, Governing Society
Social Theory, Research Policy and Environmental Transition
Alain-Marc Rieu

The Economics of Sustainable Transformation
Edited by Anna Szelągowska and Aneta Pluta-Zaremba

Planning and the Multi-local Urban Experience
The Power of Lifescapes
Kimmo Lapintie

European Port Cities and Urban Regeneration
Exploring Cultural and Sporting Mega Events at the Water's Edge
Enrico Tommarchi

Designing Smart and Resilient Cities for a Post-Pandemic World
Metropandemic Revolution
Anthony Larsson and Andreas Hatzigeorgiou

Political Geography of Cities and Regions
Changing Legitimacy and Identity
Kees Terlouw

The Economic Geography of the Car Market
The Automobile Revolution in an Emerging Economy
Edited by Bartłomiej Kołsut and Tadeusz Stryjakiewicz

Worker Mobility and Urban Policy in Latin America
Policy Interactions and Urban Outcomes in Mexico City
David López-García

For more information about this series, please visit: www.routledge.com/series/RAIRESP

Worker Mobility and Urban Policy in Latin America

Policy Interactions and Urban Outcomes in Mexico City

David López-García

Routledge
Taylor & Francis Group
LONDON AND NEW YORK

First published 2023
by Routledge
4 Park Square, Milton Park, Abingdon, Oxon OX14 4RN

and by Routledge
605 Third Avenue, New York, NY 10158

Routledge is an imprint of the Taylor & Francis Group, an informa business

British Library Cataloguing-in-Publication Data
A catalogue record for this book is available from the British Library

Library of Congress Cataloging-in-Publication Data
LC record available at https://lccn.loc.gov/2022021096

ISBN: 978-1-032-19970-2 (hbk)
ISBN: 978-1-032-19971-9 (pbk)
ISBN: 978-1-003-26169-8 (ebk)

DOI: 10.4324/9781003261698

Typeset in Bembo
by Apex CoVantage, LLC

To Ayesha and our baby girl.

Contents

Acknowledgments

Writing a book is a collective effort. I would have never been able to complete this research without the help of many generous colleagues, friends, and family who supported me during my doctoral studies. I will start by thanking my family. I am immeasurably grateful to my parents, who supported this project unconditionally from day one. Mamá, Papá, thank you for always being there for me. I am extremely grateful to my wife, Ayesha, who walked with me through ups and downs. She was always there to cheer me up and willing to discuss the ins and outs of this research. Wife, this book is as much yours as it is mine.

I thank my advisors, colleagues, and friends at The New School. I lack the words to express my gratitude to Michael Cohen for being such a generous and supportive mentor throughout my doctoral studies. I am grateful to Miodrag Mitrasinovic and David Howell for backing my research and providing detailed and substantial feedback. I also thank William Morrish, Rachel Meltzer, Margarita Gutman, Stephen Collier, Antina von Schnitzler, Óscar Sosa López, Joseph Heathcott, and Erika Kohl-Arenas, faculty at The New School who over the years shaped my work in different ways. I am also grateful to the India China Institute whose support to my research stay in China significantly influenced the way I look at Latin American cities today. To all my fellow classmates, a heartfelt thank you for your support and invaluable friendship.

Completing this research would have not been possible without the assistance of many generous people in Mexico City. I am grateful to Professor Martha Schteingart from El Colegio de México, who became a generous mentor and guided me through the challenge of conducting fieldwork in Mexico City. I thank Gian Carlo Delgado Ramos from CEIICH-UNAM who hosted me for a research stay and allowed me to organize a seminar series at UNAM to present and discuss my ongoing research. I am so grateful to Mauricio Hernández, Raquel Aguilera, and Mónica Andrade for opening their homes to me during my fieldwork. I will always treasure our days as roommates. I also thank those in Mexico City who generously provided logistical support for my fieldwork. Uzzias Martínez, Luisa Lazo, Betsy Alfaro, and Patricia Rentería, your help meant the world to me. I am grateful to Alejandro Mendoza, who with immense generosity introduced me to fascinating Ixtapaluca.

I also thank the editors at Routledge and the anonymous reviewers, as well as Professor Basilio Verduzco Chávez from the University of Guadalajara and Ryan Whitney from Tecnológico de Monterrey Campus México City for providing valuable feedback on the final version of the book manuscript. Finally, I thank the Mexican National Science and Technology Council (CONACYT); the Mexican Ministry of Education (SEP); the Julien Studley Fellowship; the Dean's Office at the Milano School of Policy, Management, and Environment; and the Office of Research Support at The New School for providing the funding for this research.

1 Introduction

Policies intended to address seemingly distinct public problems can sometimes interact and produce unintended urban outcomes. For example, infrastructure policies that provide urban amenities are likely to have an effect over land values, which will impose important challenges for the provision of affordable housing. Economic development policies that promote business improvement districts are likely to attract commuters and consumers from across an urban region, which will produce challenges for transportation policy. Public transport policy is likely to spark processes of real estate speculation around newly developed transport system stations, which will produce conflicts around land-use policy. Examples like these abound.

The policies addressing the ongoing COVID-19 pandemic showed another face of how policies can interact to produce unintended consequences. For instance, while mandatory lockdowns prevented the spread of the disease, they also put workers whose jobs needed face-to-face interaction in vulnerable positions. The lack of commuters and drop in ridership brought about by mandatory lockdowns posed important challenges for the financial sustainability of public transport systems. We are only starting to see the unintended urban consequences brought about by COVID-related policies. Only time will tell which new urban challenges will arise. This is problematic because we know very little about how policies designed to address distinct urban policy areas interact in the long run.

Contemporary urban policy analysis is based on a sectorial approach that subdivides urban dynamics into individual *policy domains*. Within this approach, scholars and practitioners have traditionally divided urban complexity into silos to analyze it and deal with it. They study and face urban problems through their own policy area. There is land-use policy, housing policy, transportation policy, economic development policy, urban health policy, public safety policy, and a long list of other policy domains. This approach to urban policy analysis has been extensively institutionalized through government structures. There are agencies in charge of specific and separate policy agendas such as planning departments, housing agencies, economic development offices, transportation departments, and so forth. The policy domains approach is widely adopted internationally across scales of urban governance at the city, metropolitan, state, and national levels.

DOI: 10.4324/9781003261698-1

The policy domains approach dominates from academic circles and higher education departments to think tanks, consulting firms, and international development agencies. Policy domains thinking is locked-in from the moment that urban development professionals are trained. For instance, transportation planners are trained in engineering departments. Housing and land-use specialists are trained in urban planning departments. Urban economists are trained in economics departments. Think tanks and consultancy firms often specialize in a focused policy area such as education, transportation, social policy, land-use planning, and so forth. In the field of international assistance for urban development, most analysis about how to face the challenges of urban settlements usually remains within disciplines and not cross-disciplines (Cohen, 2016).

The policy domains approach to urban policy analysis is problematic for at least two reasons. First, the approach leads researchers and practitioners to retreat into narrow areas of expertise, which has led to a failure to link together important subfields of investigation (Duranton & Guerra, 2016). Within this approach, for example, it is often the case that "land use specialists deal exclusively with land use, transportation planners focus only on transportation, and housing specialists think only about shelter" (Duranton & Guerra, 2016, p. 5). Second, by directing scholars' and policymakers' attention to a specific policy area, the domains approach makes it difficult to identify the policy interactions that produce spatial and social urban inequalities.

This is not to say that the discussion about policy interactions has been completely absent from scholarly debates. The public policy literature has proposed several analytical frameworks for the study of policy interactions, but none of them have been designed for urban policy analysis. The policy coherence framework, designed for the study of environmental policy, aims to provide a blueprint for achieving the coherence of policies in advancing the goals of sustainable development (Nilsson et al., 2012, 2016). The term *policy interactions* proper has been used in policy debates in three main areas, none of which is related to urban policy. First, scholars have used the term policy interactions for the study of the interaction between fiscal and monetary policy at the macroeconomic level (Azad et al., 2021; Davig & Leeper, 2011; Traum & Yang, 2011). Second, scholars of environmental policy have used the term for discussions on human-landscape systems (Gerlak, 2014), science-policy interactions (Coreau, 2020), and protected areas (Gruby et al., 2021). Third, scholars of public administration have used the term to investigate how policies that are applied concurrently might interact with each other and its effects on the frequency and quality of collaboration between organizations (Fuller & Vu, 2011). As this account conveys, the available frameworks for the study of policy interactions are thought of as analytical tools for policy design.

Over at least the past 20 years, urban studies scholars in disciplines such as geography, urban planning, and urban sociology have been calling for greater attention to how policies interact in urban settings (Bazurli, 2020; Li et al., 2014; Robinson, 2015). For instance, scholars have studied the interaction between transport and jobs (Cui et al., 2019; Niedzielski & Boschmann, 2014), transport and housing (Figueroa et al., 2018; Fuentes, 2008; Graizbord & Santillán, 2005; Schteingart & Ibarra, 2016), housing and jobs (Suárez et al., 2016; Zhao & Howden-Chapman, 2010), and even the interaction between transport, housing, and jobs (Levinson, 1998; Manaugh et al., 2010). Despite these advancements, research on how policies from distinct policy domains interact is still in its early stages and much research is still to be done. This is where I find the inspiration for this book. Standing on the shoulders of the urban studies scholarship, I argue that the cumulative effects of long-term policy interactions and their connections to unintended urban outcomes remains understudied.

Focusing policy interactions

There is an urgent need to stop thinking and practicing urban policy as if each policy domain confronts its own challenges, or as if individual policies have no impact on the way cities operate. How can we produce a shift in urban policy analysis, from the traditional policy domains approach to a broader frame of urban analyses able to go beyond the silos? How can we move beyond frameworks limited to policy design, to frameworks that allow us to identify the long-term policy interactions that have produced inequitable urban outcomes? This book proposes a reconciliation of existing theories and analytical frameworks of urban change to better understand how policy interactions lead to spatial and social unintended consequences. To do so, the *Policy Interactions Framework* (PIF) is developed and applied. The PIF constitutes an original approach to urban policy analysis designed to explore the possibility that urban outcomes are better understood as the result of the dynamics of interactions between policies from different policy domains than from any single policy silo. In doing so, the PIF provides lens to look at the cumulative effect of multiple policy decisions over time and geographic scope.

The PIF is built borrowing from three influential literatures: urban accessibility (Geurs & van Wee, 2004; Levine et al., 2019), urban political economy (Nevarez, 2015), and policy feedback theory (Mettler & Sorelle, 2017). The literature on urban accessibility investigates the extent to which land-use and transport systems enable individuals and social groups to reach the places that are fundamental for their reproduction (Geurs & van Wee, 2004; Kellerman, 2006). The field of urban political economy examines how urban development shapes and is shaped by the strategic decisions and activities from economic, social, and governmental actors (Nevarez, 2015). From the perspective of urban political economy, urban policies can be understood as the outcome of negotiation and compromise between urban actors participating in the policy process. The lens of urban political economy allows seeing that urban change is fueled with the input of specific urban actors who have their own agenda and capacity to shape policy decisions (Verduzco, 2013, 2021). Policy feedback theory holds that policies, once operating, restructure subsequent political processes by becoming an additional layer to the institutional setting within which the policy process takes place (Mettler, 2016; Mettler & Sorelle, 2017; Skocpol,

1992). The PIF, then, is designed to explore the possibility that the political economy within a specific policy domain can sometimes produce outcomes that loop back as an input into the political economy within a distinct policy domain.

The strategy for the empirical investigation of policy interactions is to study the *journey to work*. Researching the journey to work has received considerable attention from scholars as it provides a gateway to better understand several features of accessibility and equity across urban regions (Cui et al., 2019; Niedzielski & Boschmann, 2014; Sang et al., 2011; Talbot et al., 2016; Watkins, 2016; Zhao & Howden-Chapman, 2010). Studying the journey to work is a useful empirical strategy because commuting patterns in urban regions are shaped by the interactions between, at least, three kinds of policies: the economic development policies that influence the geographies of jobs, the housing policies that determine the residential location of workers, and the transport policies that provide cities with transportation systems. The study focuses on the interaction between these three policy domains. Epistemologically, it is in the study of such interaction where new knowledge about the causality between urban policy and the urban experience is produced.

There are of course policies from other policy domains that can contribute to shape the mobility experience of workers. For instance, land-use planning plays a key role because land-use decisions determine both the location of jobs and the location of housing (Verduzco, 2021). Land-use planning, economic development policies, and housing policies are closely related fields, and the sequence of decisions in this bundle plays a role on how cities produce inequalities in the mobility experience of high- and low-income workers. Education policy is another example. Policies that increase the population's educational attainment give workers access to an array of job markets spread across urban space, thus changing workers' commuting patterns. Policies from other policy domains such as fiscal and trade policies, social policy, labor policies, and environmental protection policy are likely to also play a role in shaping commuting patterns.

While I do not overlook the importance of these and other policies in shaping the mobility experience of workers, trying to investigate the interaction between the totality of policies that might interact to shape commuting would have made this investigation too ambitious and unmanageable. Aiming to narrow down the scope of the empirical investigation, and because the main goal of this book is to propose analytical refinement, I focus exclusively on the interaction between economic development, housing, and public transport policies. I leave the investigation of policies other than the selected for this study to future research endeavors.

The context: Mexico City Metropolitan Zone

This book investigates Mexico City Metropolitan Zone (MCMZ) as an attempt to regard the experience of metropolitan areas in Latin America and other emerging economies in the Global South as the ideal case study for

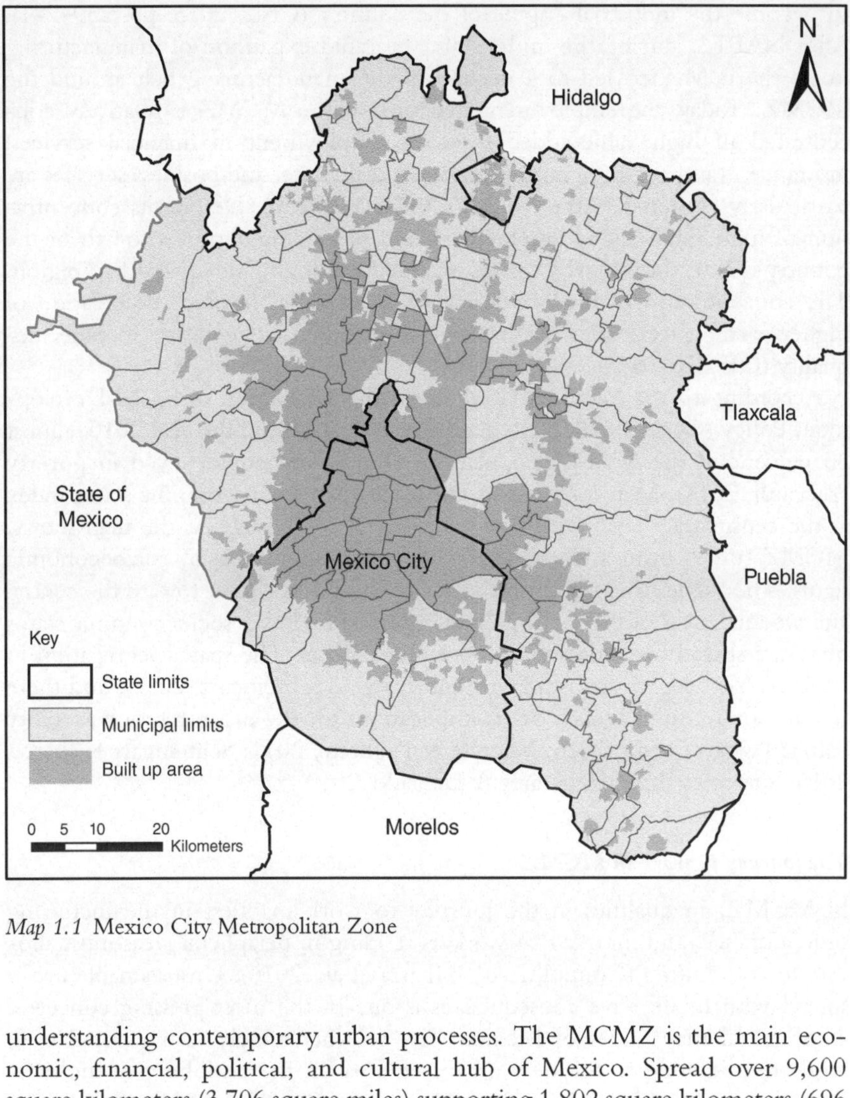

Map 1.1 Mexico City Metropolitan Zone

understanding contemporary urban processes. The MCMZ is the main economic, financial, political, and cultural hub of Mexico. Spread over 9,600 square kilometers (3,706 square miles) supporting 1,802 square kilometers (696 square miles) of built-up area, MCMZ produces 23.1 percent of the national gross domestic product (Garza, 2020) and is home to 19.4 million people (INEGI, 2021). The metropolitan region is spread over three distinct states, with 16 mayoralties (or *alcaldías* as called in Spanish) located in Mexico City (formerly known as the Federal District, or DF), 59 municipalities found in the State of Mexico (Estado de México), and one municipality located in the State of Hidalgo (Map 1.1).

Once the main industrial core of Mexico, the MCMZ is transforming its economic activity toward the service sector. After WWII, during the imports-substitution developmental period, the MCMZ industrialized rapidly to become the industrial engine of the country (Cruz, 2015: pp. 239–241). After NAFTA, during the mid-1990s, the rapid expansion of manufacturing in northern Mexico led to a decline of the manufacturing belt around the MCMZ. Today, the employment structure in the MCMZ is relatively concentrated in high value-added services. Employment in financial services, insurance, transport and communications, real estate, and business services are particularly clustered in the MCMZ (OECD, 2015b). Despite its concentration of high value-added employment and producing almost a fourth of the country's GDP, the MCMZ can be regarded as a highly unequal urban region. The concentration of high value-added services has favored the creation of higher-earning territories but has also contributed to aggravate income inequality (OECD, 2015a).

According to the National Council for the Evaluation of Social Development Policy (CONEVAL, by its acronym in Spanish), in the year 2010, almost 35 percent of the MCMZ population—7 million people—lived in poverty (Ziccardi, 2014). Map 1.2 presents the results of a socioeconomic status index at the census tract level with data from the 2020 census.[1] As the map shows, MCMZ suffers from a clear pattern of spatial segregation by socioeconomic status. The higher socioeconomic status census tracts cluster toward the central and western areas of the metropolitan region. The lower socioeconomic status tracts are spread over the east and peripheral areas. The spatial segregation in MCMZ has been widely studied (Rubalcava & Schteingart, 2012), and there is a prolific research agenda on its implications for the urban region's mobility patterns (Ibarra et al., 2016; Negrete & Paquette, 2011; Schteingart & Ibarra, 2016; Suárez et al., 2016; Suárez & Delgado, 2010).

The journey to work in MCMZ

In MCMZ, inequalities in the journey to work manifest in the increasing time, distance, and money that workers residing in peripheral areas must allocate to commuting (Connolly, 2018; Ibarra et al., 2016). Unsustainable urban sprawl with its negative consequences is one of the most pressing concerns. The central mayoralties of Mexico City are increasingly losing population, who are migrating to the new urbanized areas in the periphery of the metropolitan region (Garrocho, 1996; Negrete & Paquette, 2011). Out of the total growth of Mexico City's area between 2005 and 2010—roughly 18,000 hectares—88 percent of growth was a result of peripheral sprawl from both new formal and informal settlements (Ziccardi, 2014). Land outside the central areas is cheaper, so moving to the periphery of the MCMZ is often the only affordable solution for low-income populations and first-time home buyers. Salient among the urban development historical trajectory in the MCMZ is the scope of issues related with irregular urbanization. While it has been impossible to quantify irregular urbanization in the MCMZ, often cited approximations

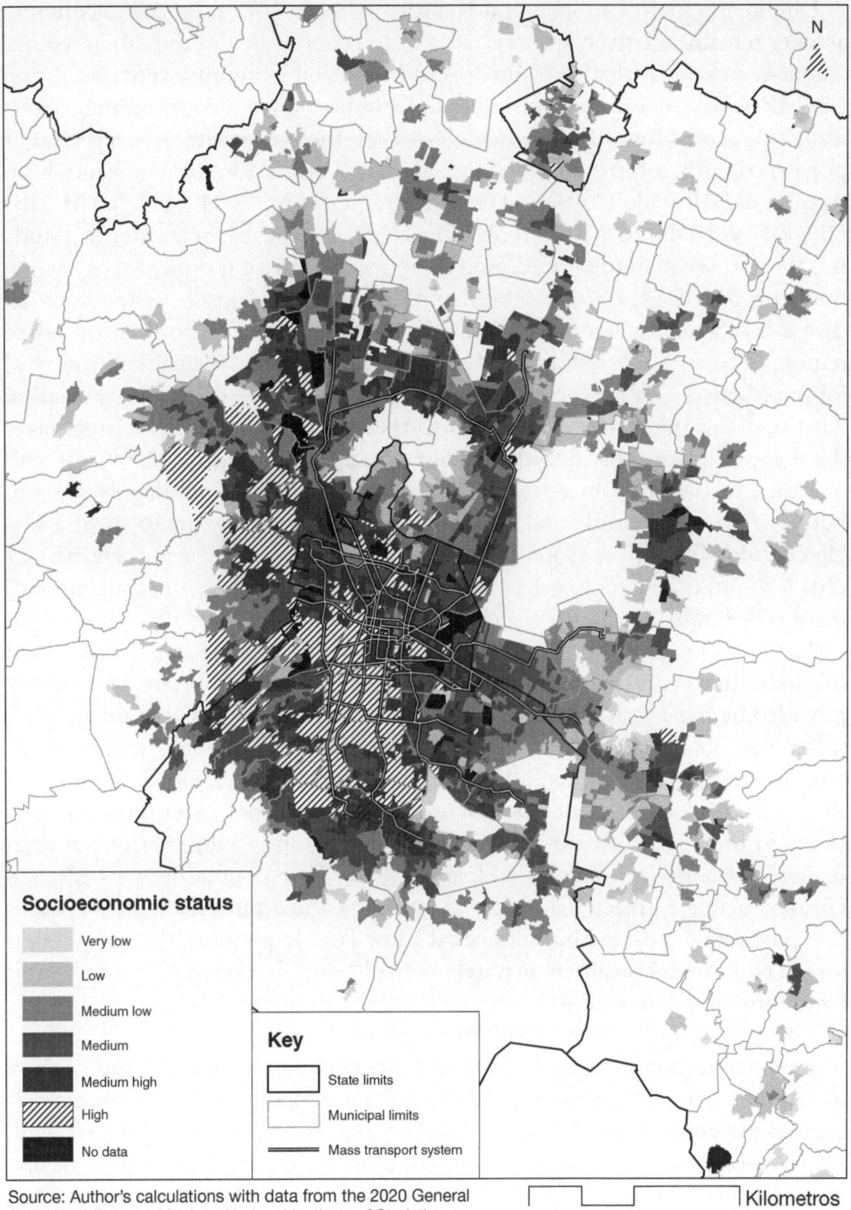

Source: Author's calculations with data from the 2020 General Population Census, Mexican National Institute of Statistics, Geography and Informatics (INEGI).

Map 1.2 Socioeconomic segregation by census tract in MCMZ, 2020 hold that between 1940 and 1970, irregular urbanization accounted for 64 percent of all new built-up area (Connolly, 2009).

Despite the intense process of urban sprawl in MCMZ, most of its economic activity remains relatively concentrated in the central area of the urban region. There is consensus that until the 70s, urban-based economic activities in the MCMZ followed a monocentric urban form but, since then, economic activity has dispersed toward subcenters. However, there is debate over the kind of polycentric urban form in which the city has evolved. On the one hand, both Aguilar and Alvarado (2004) and Graizbord and Acuña (2004) hold that Mexico City has evolved into a classic polycentric urban form. In their empirical studies, the former identified 35 dominant subcenters of economic activity while the latter found 14. On the other hand, Suárez and Delgado (2009) contend that it is difficult to ascertain that Mexico City is indeed a polycentric urban region. The authors found that over 70 percent of the formal and informal jobs in Mexico City are located within what they call the *Central Agglomeration*. That is, a very large area contiguous to the central business district that takes the shape of a large corridor. Accordingly, Suárez and Delgado (2009) contend that the Central Agglomeration in Mexico City might resemble polycentrism but has expanded linearly and concentrically through the years to amass a single corridor-like urban shape. In a subsequent study, Aguilar and Hernández (2012) found that there is a clear tendency for the appearance of more employment subcenters, but they are accruing in the central city and its adjacent area.

The new neighborhoods produced by urban sprawl are usually ill-served of public transit infrastructure and where the service does exist, it is mostly provided by the private sector and not by the state. Mexico City's urban space suffers a severe landscape of spatial injustice in the access to public transport systems (Contreras & Hidalgo, 2012; Graizbord, 2008; Islas, 2000; Schteingart & Ibarra, 2016). Government investment in public transport systems has concentrated in the central area of the metropolitan region, leaving peripheral areas in disinvestment (Schteingart & Ibarra, 2016). The central areas of Mexico City are better connected and served by state-owned public transport systems that provide subway and bus services at a low fare. In contrast, the periphery is served almost exclusively by privately owned buses that operate in a for-profit logic through a concessions system (Negrete & Paquette, 2011).

The interaction between rapid urban sprawl, severe spatial injustice in access to public transport systems, and persistent concentration of economic activity in employment subcenters is producing inequalities in the mobility experience of workers.[2] By analyzing the 2007 origin-destination survey, Ibarra et al. (2016) found that the average cost of a public transit ride increases with distance to the city center. Cervero (2013) found that in Mexico City, travel can consume 25 percent or more of daily wages and 20 percent of workers spend more than three hours traveling to and from work each day. In a comparison of transportation costs between residents of the Federal District and those of the State of Mexico, Connolly (2018) found a stark difference between the two political demarcations. The cost for a bus ride in the Federal District ranges between 0.23 and 0.46 USD, and 77 percent of the residents spend less than

20 percent of their monthly income on transportation. The average cost of a bus ride in the State of Mexico ranges between 0.54 and 3.84 USD, and only 63 percent of the population spend less than 20 percent of their monthly income on transportation. Inequalities in the mobility experience of workers can also be seen when looking at time use. Ibarra et al. (2016) found that 73.4 percent of commuters in the Federal District and 57.6 percent of commuters in the State of Mexico spend less than an hour in the trip back home. Connolly (2018) found that 7 percent of the Federal District residents spend more than three hours per day on their commutes, while this figure rises to 20 percent in the case of the State of Mexico residents.

The case study: Eastern-MCMZ

Eastern-MCMZ (or in Spanish, *Oriente de la Zona Metropolitana de la Ciudad de México*) is used as a case study for this research. The Eastern-MCMZ provides a useful research setting as it stands out for the long commutes that residents must bear and has a well-deserved reputation of being a dormitory city (or *ciudad dormitorio*, in Spanish) (Hiernaux & Lindón, 2004; Quiroz, 2013). The area of study is composed of 26 travel districts located both in the most eastern part of the mayoralty of Iztapalapa, in Mexico City, and the municipalities of Nezahualcóyotl, Chimalhuacán, La Paz, Chicoloapan, and Ixtapaluca, in the State of Mexico (Map 1.3). With 2.74 million inhabitants (INEGI, 2021), Eastern-MCMZ is home to 14.1 percent of MCMZ's population.

Table 1.1 shows some of the land-use, transport, and socioeconomic characteristics of Eastern-MCMZ and puts the case study area in perspective with all travel districts within the MCMZ. Land-use patterns between MCMZ and Eastern-MCMZ differ significantly. Eastern-MCMZ offers significantly fewer jobs to their inhabitants than the rest of the urban region. While in MCMZ job density is 30.9 jobs per hectare and job/housing balance is one job per each housing unit, the figures go down to 16.9 and 0.39 in Eastern-MCMZ, respectively. Average distance from the centroid of each travel district to the closest mass transport station is 2.8 km for Eastern-MCMZ and 4.2 km for the MCMZ. Map 1.3 shows that there are two mass transport systems serving Eastern-MCMZ's population. The first, Line A of the subway system, operates since 1991 and serves the southern area of Eastern-MCMZ in the limits between Mexico City and the State of Mexico. The second, operating since 2013, is Line 3 of the State of Mexico Bus Rapid Transit (BRT) Mexibús that serves the northern area of Eastern-MCMZ. The transportation needs of the population beyond the service area of these two mass transport systems are met by private providers of minibuses services. Eastern-MCMZ is also served by CETRAM Pantitlán (Map 1.3), the most proximate transportation hub with four subway lines connecting commuters with the rest of the urban region.

Previous studies of socioeconomic segregation in MCMZ have pointed out how the Eastern territory of the metropolitan region has consistently been a disadvantaged territory (Rubalcava & Schteingart, 2012). Table 1.1 puts the socioeconomic characteristics of Eastern-MCMZ in perspective with the rest of

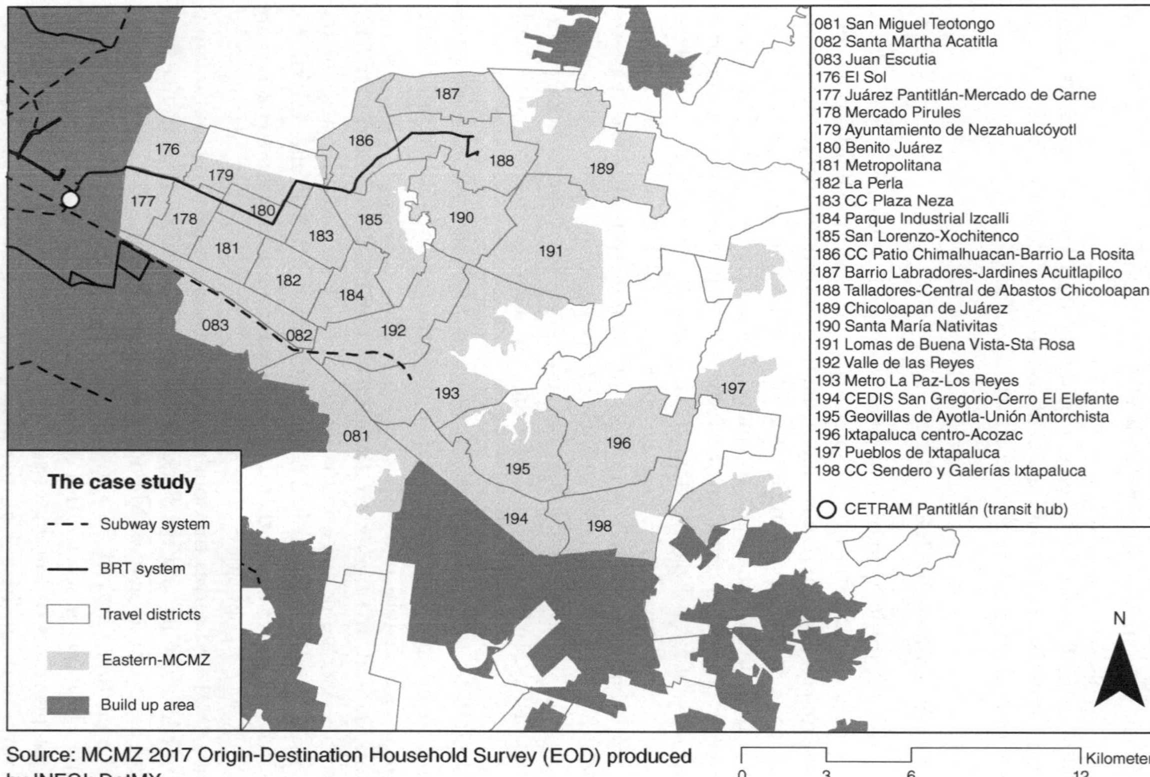

Source: MCMZ 2017 Origin-Destination Household Survey (EOD) produced by INEGI; DotMX.

Map 1.3 The case study: Eastern-MCMZ

Table 1.1 Land-use, transport, and socioeconomic characteristics of Eastern-MCMZ

District	*State*	*Municipality*	*Job density (Jobs/Ha)**	*Job/housing balance**	*Distance to mass public transport station (km)***	*Years of schooling**	*Population employed (%)**	*Population with benefits (%)**	*SES 2020****
081	Mexico City	Iztapalapa	15.2	0.31	2.0	9.4	62.2	28.8	0.64
082	Mexico City	Iztapalapa	20.7	0.47	0.6	10.6	62.5	37.9	0.71
083	Mexico City	Iztapalapa	15.1	0.49	1.1	9.8	62.6	30.7	0.67
176	State of Mexico	Nezahualcoyotl	16.3	0.30	1.2	9.9	61.3	33.8	0.66
177	State of Mexico	Nezahualcoyotl	24.4	0.38	0.8	10.2	61.9	36.3	0.68
178	State of Mexico	Nezahualcoyotl	25.7	0.41	0.8	10.6	62.4	35.7	0.70
179	State of Mexico	Nezahualcoyotl	22.4	0.38	0.7	10.1	62.6	35.5	0.68
180	State of Mexico	Nezahualcoyotl	27.0	0.40	0.3	10.3	61.5	34.7	0.69
181	State of Mexico	Nezahualcoyotl	30.0	0.50	1.2	10.5	61.6	34.5	0.70
182	State of Mexico	Nezahualcoyotl	22.3	0.37	1.7	10.1	61.4	32.6	0.68
183	State of Mexico	Nezahualcoyotl	22.9	0.37	1.6	10.0	62.2	31.4	0.67
184	State of Mexico	Nezahualcoyotl	21.0	0.45	2.1	10.0	60.9	32.6	0.66
185	State of Mexico	Chimalhuacán	12.4	0.26	1.8	9.3	61.7	28.2	0.62
186	State of Mexico	Chimalhuacán	17.5	0.34	0.9	9.2	62.0	27.8	0.62
187	State of Mexico	Chimalhuacán	12.7	0.25	1.4	8.8	62.6	24.5	0.58
188	State of Mexico	Chimalhuacán/ Chicoloapan	13.0	0.35	0.6	9.5	63.4	31.3	0.62
189	State of Mexico	Chicoloapan/ Texcoco	7.9	0.27	5.1	10.4	62.9	46.2	0.67
190	State of Mexico	Chimalhuacán/ Chicoloapan	11.4	0.38	2.4	9.2	62.4	28.3	0.60
191	State of Mexico	Chimalhuacán/ Chicoloapan	10.8	0.34	3.8	9.1	61.7	31.7	0.58
192	State of Mexico	La Paz	23.8	0.63	1.5	9.9	62.9	33.4	0.65

(*Continued*)

Table 1.1 (Continued)

District	*State*	*Municipality*	*Job density (Jobs/Ha)**	*Job/housing balance**	*Distance to mass public transport station (km)***	*Years of schooling**	*Population employed (%)**	*Population with benefits (%)**	*SES 2020****
193	State of Mexico	La Paz	11.2	0.48	2.2	9.4	63.3	33.8	0.61
194	State of Mexico	Ixtapaluca/Valle de Chalco S.	11.7	0.42	5.2	9.7	62.3	35.0	0.65
195	State of Mexico	Ixtapaluca	11.9	0.32	4.8	9.7	62.7	40.0	0.64
196	State of Mexico	Ixtapaluca	11.4	0.32	8.4	10.4	62.7	47.5	0.68
197	State of Mexico	Ixtapaluca	7.1	0.25	12.8	10.2	60.5	35.1	0.65
198	State of Mexico	Ixtapaluca	14.7	0.75	8.5	10.8	62.0	45.7	0.70
All travel districts in MCMZ			16.9	0.39	2.8	9.9	62.2	34.3	0.65
All travel districts in Eastern-MCM			30.9	1.0	4.2	10.8	62.9	43.6	0.70

Source: * 2020 General Census, INEGI; ** Author's calculations based on public transport GIS layers from DotMX; ***Author's calculations with data from the 2020 General Census, INEGI travel districts in MCMZ. While the socioeconomic status index for MCMZ is 0.7, the index goes down to 0.65 for travel districts within the case study. The population in Eastern-MCMZ has in average one less year of schooling than the population in all travel districts within MCMZ. Most saliently, workers in Eastern-MCMZ have more access to formal jobs than workers across the urban region. While the percentage of population employed is quite similar—62.2 and 62.9 in MCMZ and Eastern-MCMZ, respectively—the percentage of population with work benefits is 34.3 in MCMZ and goes up to 43.6 in the case of Eastern-MCMZ. Given that most formal jobs cluster toward the center, west, and northwest of the urban region (see Chapter 4), increased access to formal jobs means that the workforce in Eastern-MCMZ must commute long distances daily to reach the places where jobs are concentrated.

Researching policy interactions

This study is based on a mixed-methods research approach to investigate current inequalities in the journey to work in MCMZ and the policy interactions that have produced such inequalities in the first place. The quantitative component of the study is based on several statistical analyses. A study of average time and distance in the journey to work identifies the spatial distribution of existing commuting inequalities. An analysis of employment subcenters between 1999 and 2019 assesses the shift in the spatial location of the demand for labor and allows identifying the places that attract most commuters. The calculation and mapping of an access to public transport index examines the spatial distribution of state-owned and state-subsidized mobility resources available to workers. Quantitative data sources used in the study include the MCMZ 2017 Origin-Destination Household Survey, the 1999 and 2019 Economic Census, the 2020 General Population Census, and the 2016 National Housing Inventory, all of them produced by Mexico's National Institute of Statistics, Geography and Informatics (INEGI); the Mexico City Open Data Portal; and the dotmx database, produced by the Institute for Transportation and Development Policy (ITDP) Mexico office. The specific data and methodology used for each empirical study are explained in detail in their corresponding chapter.

The qualitative component of the study is based on fieldwork in MCMZ done over several field immersions. The first took place in the Fall of 2018 through a research stay at the Center for Interdisciplinary Research in the Sciences and Humanities (CEIICH) of the National Autonomous University of Mexico (UNAM). Several other field immersions took place between April and July of 2019, when I returned to Mexico City on different occasions to collect missing pieces of data. In total, 64 in-depth interviews with key informants and four focus groups with 30 residents from the area of study were conducted.[3] The in-depth interviews took place among two groups of key informants. The first group was composed of 33 policy-related informants coming from urban development and transportation experts, government officials, civil society organizations, and academia. The second group of interviewees was composed of 31 residents of Eastern-MCMZ. The sampling strategy for the in-depth interviews consisted of snowballing, with initial participants of the study connecting me with other potential participants until a saturation point was reached. The focus groups were conducted with residents from the mayoralty of Iztapalapa in Mexico City, and municipalities of Nezahualcóyotl, Chimalhuacán, and Ixtapaluca in the State of Mexico. Audio recordings from each of the in-depth interviews and the focus groups were transcribed and analyzed inductively with the support of the analytical lenses that will be presented in the next chapter.

Research findings and contributions

In MCMZ, there are severe spatial inequalities in the mobility experience of workers through public transport. Average commuting time ranges from 42.9 to 104.6 minutes. Average commuting distance ranges from 4.7 to 30.7 kilometers. Commuters in the 90th percentile of the distribution need 1.71 and 2.65 times the average time and distance, respectively, than commuters in the 10th percentile. The spatial distribution of mobility situations shows a concentric pattern, with the shortest commutes located in the central and western areas of the MCMZ and the longest commutes in peripheral areas. Eastern-MCMZ, the case study for this book, has one of the costliest mobility experiences in terms of time and distance allocated to commuting.

The demand for labor in MCMZ is concentrating in space. Despite the appearance of new employment subcenters, from 22 in 1999 to 29 in 2019, and a primacy index showing a trend toward a polycentric urban form, from 3.44 in 1999 to 2.26 in 2019, the formal jobs available in MCMZ keep concentrating in less territory. In 1999, 52.8 percent of the jobs available in the metropolitan region were concentrated in 9.3 percent of its territory. By 2019, 58.5 percent of the jobs were concentrated in 8.4 percent of the territory. Furthermore, most of the new employment subcenters and those moving up in the urban hierarchy are in the center, west, and northwest of the metropolitan region. The shift in the geographies of jobs keeps operating to the disadvantage of the population residing in Eastern-MCMZ.

Housing policies in MCMZ are producing default housing pathways that are consistently increasing the physical separation between jobs and workers. Workers do not just choose to live in geographies of low accessibility to jobs; they live in such territories due to default housing pathways and the lack of alternatives. There is a relationship between the types of jobs that workers have access to and the housing pathways that become available for them. Default housing pathways, in turn, contribute to shape specific mobility situations for workers. The study allowed to identify three ideal types of mobility situations: (i) the mobility experience based on the use value of housing, (ii) the mobility experience based on the national housing policy, and (iii) the mobility experience based on access to primary labor markets.

As per public transport, the distribution of state-owned and state-subsidized mobility resources in MCMZ is strikingly unequal. For example, 70.3 percent of the territory of MCMZ has no state-funded public transport system at all, 24 percent has a low or medium-low provision, 4.1 percent has medium provision, and only 1.7 percent of the urban region's territory has a medium-high or high provision. Not surprisingly, virtually all the areas that are well-served of state-funded public transport systems are in the central areas of the metropolitan region and overlap with existing employment subcenters. Eastern-MCMZ has a very low provision of publicly funded mobility resources. The increasing mobility needs of workers in Eastern-MCMZ are met mainly by private providers of public transport through systems that are highly fragmented and commodified.

One of the main contributions of this study is the PIF, which provides analytical and methodological tools for the empirical investigation of policy interactions in urban settings. The PIF is developed in Chapter 2, where a step-by-step guide on how to use it is provided. The application of the PIF to the study of the journey to work in MCMZ demonstrates that the highly unequal mobility experience of workers is the result of the interaction between three urban policy domains that often work at cross-purposes: economic development, housing, and transportation.

Two specific policy interactions were identified. The first has to do with the intense urbanization of Eastern-MCMZ and the emergence of private providers of public transport and their organizations as powerful political actors. In the absence of the state to provide public transport systems, the population's mobility needs have produced a new source of urban wealth because workers must pay to satisfy their mobility requirements. This new source of urban wealth was up for grabs, and private providers of public transport and their organizations called *transportistas* (transporters) mobilized to capture it. Over time, the *transportistas* have constituted themselves into powerful political organizations with important influence over public transport policy. The second policy interaction has to do with economic development and housing policies interacting to increase the transportation costs for workers in Eastern-MCMZ. On one hand, economic development policies have concentrated jobs in employment subcenters toward the center, west, and northwest of the MCMZ. On the other hand, housing policies have pulled a considerable share of workers further into Eastern-MCMZ. While the interaction between economic development and housing policies is consistently increasing the physical separation between jobs and workers, the commodification and fragmentation of public transport systems are increasing the transportation costs for workers.

Lastly, the book develops and puts forward the choiceless mobility hypothesis (CMH), which I define as the process through which the interaction between policies from distinct policy domains produce mobility situations that consistently increase the transportation costs for workers (Figure 1.1).

The CMH is composed of the following elements. First, urban regions can experience a long-term process of spatial structuring in which the interaction

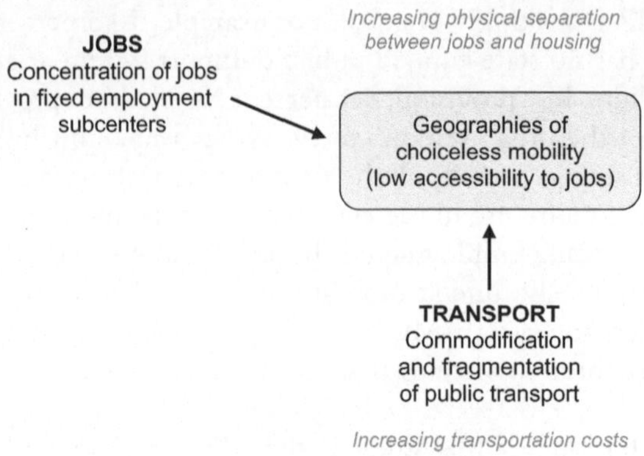

Figure 1.1 The choiceless mobility hypothesis

between (i) the spatial location patterns in the demand for labor, (ii) the housing pathways available for workers, and (iii) the political economy of public transport operates to produce geographies of low accessibility to jobs. Second, the interaction between the concentration of jobs in specific employment subcenters and the production of housing for workers in peripheral areas can increase the physical separation between workers and jobs and therefore increase the workers' mobility needs. Amid a landscape of commodification and fragmentation of public transport systems, the increasing mobility needs of workers increase their transportation costs. And third, workers do not just *choose* to live in low-accessibility territories. Instead, they have no option but to live in such territories due to the lack of alternatives and default housing pathways. The CMH occurs when the economic activities in which workers participate is concentrating in space, while the default housing pathways that are available for workers keep increasing their transportation costs.

Structure of the book

This book is structured as follows. Chapter 2 presents the theoretical framework developed for the study: the Policy Interactions Framework (PIF). The framework allows stepping out of the traditional policy domains approach in urban policy analysis to investigate the interactions between public policies from distinct policy silos. Additionally, the framework provides analytical lenses to identify the production of specific accessibility outcomes. After an overview of the literature on accessibility, urban political economy, and policy feedback theory, the chapter builds on each of these bodies of literature to assemble the PIF. The chapter ends with a step-by-step guide on how to apply the framework.

Chapter 3 investigates the average time and distance of the journey to work in MCMZ as a gateway to evaluating inequalities in the mobility situations of workers. The chapter analyzes a subsample of the 2017 Origin-Destination Survey to calculate the time and distance of the journey to work across a sample of 194 travel districts. By replicating available methodologies (Niedzielski & Boschmann, 2014), the chapter groups travel districts into four distinct mobility situations according to whether their average time and distance falls above or below the metropolitan average: (i) Long Commutes: districts above the city average in both time and distance; (ii) Short Commutes: districts below the average in both time and distance; (iii) Wormholes: districts below the average time but above the average distance; and (iv) Transit Hells: districts above the average time but below the average distance. The mobility situations are then mapped, which allows one to observe spatial inequalities in the mobility situations of workers.

Chapter 4 argues that shifts in the spatial location of the demand for labor partially determines the mobility experience of workers. Accordingly, the chapter presents an empirical study of such shift in MCMZ between 1999 and 2019. The chapter conducts an analysis of employment magnitude and density to identify employment subcenters, assesses the economic specialization and the type of jobs available in each subcenter, and evaluates whether the MCMZ trends toward a polycentric or a monocentric urban structure. The study shows that, despite MCMZ generating more employment subcenters, jobs are consistently concentrating in less space around the central and western area of the metropolitan region.

Chapter 5 investigates why workers live in geographies of low accessibility to jobs in the first place. The chapter presents an empirical study of the relationship between housing pathways and the mobility experience of workers in Eastern-MCMZ. Based on semi-structured interviews with residents of the area of study, the chapter identifies three distinct ideal types of relationships between housing pathways and workers' mobility experiences: housing use value-based, national housing policy-based, and access to labor market-based. The study shows a relationship between the types of jobs to which workers have access, the housing pathways available for them, and their mobility experience. The chapter concludes by arguing that workers do not just choose to live in geographies of low accessibility. Instead, residents live in such territories due to their default housing pathways and the lack of alternatives.

One of the prerequisites to be mobile across urban space is to have access to mobility resources. Chapter 6 takes a political economy approach to assess the extent to which publicly funded mobility resources are equitably distributed across the urban region. The chapter proposes an analytical framework based on evaluating the levels of rivalry and excludability of mobility resources. This analytical framework maps the spatial distribution of what I call public and common mobility resources across MCMZ. The study shows that publicly funded mobility resources in MCMZ tend to overlap with existing employment subcenters while leaving peripheral areas in disinvestment.

Finally, Chapter 7 takes a comprehensive look at the four empirical studies presented in this book and analyzes them through the Policy Interactions

Framework (PIF). Two specific policy interactions are identified and analyzed. The first has to do with housing policy, the intense urbanization of Eastern-MCMZ, and the emergence of private providers of public transport and their organizations as powerful political actors with important influence in public transport policy. The second policy interaction has to do with economic development and housing policies interacting to increase the transportations costs for workers in Eastern-MCMZ. As an outcome of applying the PIF, the chapter develops and puts forward the *choiceless mobility hypothesis* (CMH). The CMH is defined as the process through which the interaction between policies from distinct policy domains produce mobility situations that consistently increase the transportation costs for workers. The chapter provides a detailed discussion of how the CMH is different from other concepts available in the literature and ends with a discussion about the implications of the CMH for urban policy analysis.

Notes

1 The strategy to assess socioeconomic segregation in MCMZ is based on replicating the methodology used by Rubalcava and Schteingart (2012) in their influential book *Ciudades Divididas*. By analyzing census data for 2020, a factor analysis regression was done, and two factors were identified. Factor 1 can be called *purchasing power* and includes four indicators: percentage of population in the labor force, average schooling years, overcrowding, and percentage of households with Internet connection. Factor 1 explains 56.7 percent of the variation in the data. Factor 2 can be called *neighborhood characteristics* and includes two indicators: percentage of households with water in the premises and percentage of households with floor material other than dirt. Factor 2 explains 20.5 percent of the variation in the data. Together, the factors can explain 77.2 percent of the variation in the selected indicators.

2 The term *mobility experience* must be clearly defined. In the literature about the journey to work, the term *mobility* has been traditionally associated with the physical movement of entities from an origin to a destination along an specific trajectory described in terms of space and time (Kaufmann et al., 2004). The word *experience* is a polysemic term, but in this book, experience is understood as something personally encountered, undergone, or lived through. In this book, then, the term *mobility experience* is defined as the way in which workers live through the physical movement from their place of residence to their place of work in terms of space and time.

3 The ethics of this research project were overseen by the Human Research Protection Program (HRPP) at The New School under Protocol #2019–1009. The HRPP granted an *exemption from the IRB review* category to this research project. Recruitment procedures, informed consent processes and documentation, research procedures, data storage, and the measures taken to secure the privacy and confidentiality and mitigate any potential risks to participants were approved by The New School's HRPP.

References

Aguilar, A., & Alvarado, C. (2004). La reestructuración del espacio urbano en la Ciudad de México. ¿Hacia una metrópoli multinodal? In A. Aguilar (Ed.), *Procesos Metropolitanos y Grandes Ciudades. Dinámicas Recientes en México y Otros Países*. Ciudad de México: Miguel Ángel Porrúa.

Aguilar, A., & Hernández, J. (2012). Transformación metropolitana y estructura policéntrica en la Ciudad de México. Identificación de subcentros urbanos, 1990–2005. In A. Ziccardi (Ed.), *Ciudades del 2010: Entre la sociedad del conocimiento y la desigualdad social*. Ciudad de México: Universidad Nacional Autónoma de México.

Azad, N. F., Serletis, A., & Xu, L. (2021). Covid-19 and monetary – fiscal policy interactions in Canada. *Quarterly Review of Economics and Finance, 81*, 376–384.

Bazurli, R. (2020). How urban is urban policy making? *PS – Political Science and Politics, 53*(1), 25–28.

Cervero, R. (2013). Linking urban transport and land use in developing countries. *Journal of Transport and Land Use, 6*(1), 7–24.

Cohen, M. A. (2016). From Habitat II to Pachamama: A growing agenda and diminishing expectations for Habitat III. *Environment and Urbanization, 28*(1), 35–48.

Connolly, P. (2009). Observing the evolution of irregular settlements: Mexico City's colonias populares, 1990 to 2005. *International Development Planning Review, 31*(1), 1–35.

Connolly, P. (2018). ¿Qué se gobierno en materia de transporte y movilidad? El caso de la Ciudad de México. In V. Ugalde & P. Le Galès (Eds.), *Gobernando la Ciudad de México: Lo que se Gobierna y lo que no se Gobierna en una gran metrópoli*. Ciudad de México: El Colegio de México.

Contreras, G., & Hidalgo, H. (2012). Justicia espacial, accesibilidad y proximidad a los elementos físicos que posibilitan la movilidad urbana en la Ciudad de México. In M. Cruz (Ed.), *Periferias Metropolitanas, Políticas Públicas y Medio Ambiente*. Ciudad de México: Universidad Autónoma Metropolitana.

Coreau, A. (2020). Reflexive strategic action to consolidate a research – NGO partnership during science – policy interactions. *Environmental Science and Policy, 113*, 55–63.

Cruz, F. (2015). *Configuración espacial de la industria en la Ciudad de México*. Ciudad de México: El Colegio de México.

Cui, B., Boisjoly, G., El-Geneidy, A., & Levinson, D. (2019). Accessibility and the journey to work through the lens of equity. *Journal of Transport Geography, 74*, 269–277.

Davig, T., & Leeper, E. M. (2011). Monetary-fiscal policy interactions and fiscal stimulus. *European Economic Review, 55*(2), 211–227.

Duranton, G., & Guerra, E. (2016). Developing a common narrative on urban accessibility: An urban planning perspective. In *Brookings: Moving to access*. Washington, D.C.: The Brookings Institution.

Figueroa, C., Hodgson, F., Mullen, C., & Timms, P. (2018). Creating inequality in accessibility: The relationships between public transport and social housing policy in deprived areas of Santiago de Chile. *Journal of Transport Geography, 67*, 102–109.

Fuentes, C. M. (2008). La estructura urbana y las diferencias espaciales en el tiempo de traslado del viaje al trabajo en Ciudad Juárez, Chihuahua. *Estudios Demográficos y Urbanos, 23*(1), 55–81.

Fuller, B. W., & Vu, K. M. (2011). Exploring the dynamics of policy interaction: Feedback among and impacts from multiple, concurrently applied policy approaches for promoting collaboration. *Journal of Policy Analysis and Management, 30*(2), 359–380.

Garrocho, C. (1996). Distributión espacial de la población en la Zona Metropolitana de la Ciudad de México, 1950–1990. *Estudios Demográficos y Urbanos, 11*(1), 69–100.

Garza, G. (2020). *Dinámica y configuración macroeconómica de la Ciudad de México, 1960–2013: Estrategia económico-espacial para la planeación multidimensional de la Ciudad de México, 2020–2040*. Ciudad de México: Comisión Económica para América Latina y el Caribe (CEPAL).

Gerlak, A. K. (2014). Policy interactions in human-landscape systems. *Environmental Management, 53*(1), 67–75.

Geurs, K. T., & van Wee, B. (2004). Accessibility evaluation of land-use and transport strategies: Review and research directions. *Journal of Transport Geography, 12*(2), 127–140.

Graizbord, B. (2008). *Geografía del transporte público en el área metropolitana de la Ciudad de México*. Ciudad de México: El Colegio de México.

Graizbord, B., & Acuña, B. (2004). La estructura polinuclear del Área Metropolitana de la Ciudad de México. In A. Aguilar (Ed.), *Procesos Metropolitanos y Grandes Ciudades. Dinámicas Recientes en México y Otros Países*. Ciudad de México: Miguel Ángel Porrúa.

Graizbord, B., & Santillán, M. (2005). Dinámica demográfica y generación de viajes al trabajo en el AMCM : 1994–2000. *Estudios Demográficos y Urbanos, 20*(1), 71–101.

Gruby, R. L., Gray, N. J., Fairbanks, L., Havice, E., Campbell, L. M., Friedlander, A., Oleson, K. L. L., Sam, K., Mitchell, L., & Hanich, Q. (2021). Policy interactions in large-scale marine protected areas. *Conservation Letters, 14*(1), 1–9.

Hiernaux, D., & Lindón, A. (2004). La periferia: Voz y sentido en los estudios urbanos. *Papeles de Población, 10*(42), 101–123.

Ibarra, V., Negrete, M. E., & Graizbord, B. (2016). Tres aristas de un mismo problema: Movilidad diferencial en la Ciudad de México. In M. E. Negrete (Ed.), *Urbanización y política urbana en Iberoamérica: Experiencias, análisis y reflexiones*. Ciudad de México: El Colegio de México.

INEGI. (2021). Censo de Población y Vivienda 2020. México: Instituto Nacional de Estadística, Geografía e Informática.

Islas, V. (2000). *Llegando tarde al compromiso*. Ciudad de México: El Colegio de México.

Kaufmann, V., Bergman, M. M., & Joye, D. (2004). Motility: Mobility as capital. *International Journal of Urban and Regional Research, 28*(4), 745–756.

Kellerman, A. (2006). *Personal mobilities*. New York and London: Routledge.

Levine, J., Grengs, J., & Merlin, L. A. (2019). *From mobility to accessibility: Transforming urban transportation and land-use planning*. Ithaca: Cornell University Press.

Levinson, D. (1998). Accessibility and the journey to work. *Journal of Transport Geography, 6*(1), 11–21.

Li, L. H., Lin, J., Li, X., & Wu, F. (2014). Redevelopment of urban village in China – A step towards an effective urban policy? A case study of Liede village in Guangzhou. *Habitat International, 43*, 299–308.

Manaugh, K., Miranda-Moreno, L. F., & El-Geneidy, A. M. (2010). The effect of neighbourhood characteristics, accessibility, home-work location, and demographics on commuting distances. *Transportation, 37*(4), 627–646.

Mettler, S. (2016). The policyscape and the challenges of contemporary politics to policy maintenance. *Perspectives on Politics, 14*(2), 369–390.

Mettler, S., & Sorelle, M. (2017). Policy feedback theory. In C. M. Weible & P. Sabatie (Eds.), *Theories of the policy process* (4th ed.). New York and London: Routledge.

Negrete, M. E., & Paquette, C. (2011). La interacción entre transporte público y urbanización en la Zona Metropolitana de la Ciudad de México un modelo expansivo que llega a sus límites. *Territorios, 25*, 15–33.

Nevarez, L. (2015). Urban political economy. In *The Blackwell Encyclopedia of Sociology*. Hoboken, NJ: John Wiley & Sons, Ltd.

Niedzielski, M. A., & Boschmann, E. E. (2014). Travel time and distance as relative accessibility in the journey to work. *Annals of the Association of American Geographers, 104*, 1156–1182.

Nilsson, M., Griggs, D., & Visbeck, M. (2016). Policy: Map the interactions between Sustainable Development Goals. *Nature, 534*, 320–322.

Nilsson, M., Zamparutti, T., Petersen, J. E., Nykvist, B., Rudberg, P., & Mcguinn, J. (2012). Understanding policy coherence: Analytical framework and examples of sector-environment policy interactions in the EU. *Environmental Policy and Governance, 22*(6), 395–423.

OECD. (2015a). *Estudios Territoriales de la OCDE Valle de México, México. Síntesis del estudio.* Paris: OECD Publishing.

OECD. (2015b). *OECD territorial reviews: Valle de México, Mexico.* Paris: OECD Publishing.

Quiroz, H. (2013). Elementos para una teoría de la ciudad mexicana contemporánea desde la práctica urbanística. *Andamios, Revista de Investigación Social, 10*(22), 113–128.

Robinson, J. (2015). "Arriving At" urban policies: The topological spaces of urban policy mobility. *International Journal of Urban and Regional Research, 39*(4), 831–834.

Rubalcava, R. M., & Schteingart, M. (2012). *Ciudades divididas: Desigualdad y segregación social en México.* Ciudad de México: El Colegio de México.

Sang, S., O'Kelly, M., & Kwan, M. P. (2011). Examining commuting patterns: Results from a journey-to-work model disaggregated by gender and occupation. *Urban Studies, 48*(5), 891–909.

Schteingart, M., & Ibarra, V. (2016). *Desarrollo urbano-ambiental y movilidad en la Ciudad de México: Evaluación histórica, cambios recientes y políticas públicas.* Ciudad de México: El Colegio de México.

Skocpol, T. (1992). *Protecting soldiers and mothers: The political origins of social policy in the United States.* Cambridge: Belkman Press of Harvard University Press.

Suárez, M., & Delgado, J. (2009). Is Mexico City polycentric? A trip attaction capacity approach. *Urban Studies, 46*(10), 2187–2211.

Suárez, M., & Delgado, J. (2010). Patrones de movilidad residencial en la ciudad de México como evidencia de co-localización de población y empleos. *Eure, 36*(107), 67–71.

Suárez, M., Murata, M., & Delgado Campos, J. (2016). Why do the poor travel less? Urban structure, commuting and economic informality in Mexico City. *Urban Studies, 53*(12), 2548–2566.

Talbot, R., Rackliff, L., Nicolle, C., Maguire, M., & Mallaband, R. (2016). Journey to work: Exploring difficulties, solutions, and the impact of aging. *International Journal of Sustainable Transportation ISSN:, 10*(6), 541–551.

Traum, N., & Yang, S. C. S. (2011). Monetary and fiscal policy interactions in the post-war U.S. *European Economic Review, 55*(1), 140–164.

Verduzco, B. (2013). *Una utopía urbana (im)posible. La negociación infinita de planes de desarrollo urbano y prosperidad.* Guadalajara: Universidad de Guadalajara.

Verduzco, B. (2021). *Extraterrenal: Cómo hacerse de una casa con o sin ayuda del gobierno.* Guadalajara: Academia Jaliscience de Ciencias, A.C.

Watkins, A. R. (2016). Commuting flows and labour market structure: Modelling journey to work behaviour in an urban environment. *Growth and Change, 47*(4), 612–630.

Zhao, P., & Howden-Chapman, P. (2010). Social inequalities in mobility: The impact of the hukou system on migrants' job accessibility and commuting costs in Beijing. *International Development Planning Review, 32*(3), 363–384.

Ziccardi, A. (2014). Poverty and urban inequality: The case of Mexico city metropolitan region. *International Social Science Journal, 65*(217–218), 205–219.

2 The Policy Interactions Framework

The world is increasingly urbanizing, and the administration of urban areas is growing in complexity. As a result, urban policy is winning relevance as a field of study and policy analysis (Bazurli, 2020; McCann, 2008; Robinson, 2015). Nevertheless, the mainstream analytical frameworks in the public policy literature have not been designed to deal with the complexity of urban areas. Urban policy analysis is based on a policy domains approach that subdivides urban dynamics into individual silos such as health, environment, education, transportation, and so forth (Cohen, 2016; Crawford, 2018). Within this approach, urban policy scholars focus on the study of one discrete policy domain, tracing it from origins to outcomes largely in isolation from other policy settings. This is problematic because the policy domains approach was not designed to deal with the complexity of urban areas. In cities, policies from distinct policy domains overlap in urban space and interact in complex ways to produce a range of urban consequences, both intended and unintended. Consequently, there is a mismatch between the available analytical frameworks from public policy analysis and the needs of urban policy to understand the knot of complex interactions among varied policies.

This chapter introduces the analytical framework developed for the study: the Policy Interactions Framework (PIF). The PIF is designed as an analytical strategy to step out of the traditional policy domains approach in urban policy analysis. The PIF facilitates the empirical investigation of how policies from distinct policy domains overlap in urban space and interact to produce specific accessibility outcomes. The PIF provides an analytical lens to explore the possibility that urban outcomes are better understood as the result of the dynamics of interactions between policies from distinct policy domains than from any single policy silo. The PIF borrows from three bodies of literature: accessibility, urban political economy, and policy feedback theory. In what follows, I present a review of the elements from each of these literatures that are used to assemble the PIF. Then, I introduce the framework, its constitutive elements, and main assumptions. The chapter ends with a step-by-step guide on how to apply the PIF for the empirical investigation of the policy interactions in urban settings.

DOI: 10.4324/9781003261698-2

Urban accessibility

Cities provide a wide array of resources to their inhabitants such as schools, hospitals, green spaces, jobs, governmental services, consumer goods, and alike. But there is a problem. Given that these resources are not evenly distributed throughout urban space, and given people's residential location and socioeconomic condition, not everyone has the same level of accessibility to such resources. Acknowledging this problem, scholars have called to put *accessibility* at the center of our thinking about urban development (Duranton & Guerra, 2016; Geurs & van Wee, 2004; Levine et al., 2019; Páez et al., 2012; van Wee & Geurs, 2011). According to these scholars, accessibility is the main urban quantity to consider from a resource allocation standpoint as it can link discussions on land use, housing, transportation, and equity (Cui et al., 2019; Duranton & Guerra, 2016).

The concept of accessibility as most of the contemporary scholars use it today was put forward by Geurs and van Wee (2004). In their influential work, Geurs and van Wee (2004) defined accessibility as "the extent to which land-use and transport systems enable (groups of) individuals to reach activities or destinations by means of a (combination of) transport mode(s)" (2004, p. 128). Following this effort, scholars have defined accessibility as the ease of reaching destinations (Duranton & Guerra, 2016); the ease of social groups and individuals to travel and reach the places that are fundamental for their reproduction (Kellerman, 2006, as cited in Calonge, 2018, p. 51); or as "the ease with which a person can reach places and opportunities from a given location" (Pereira et al., 2019, p. 746). To Handy and Niemeier (1997), accessibility is determined by "the spatial distribution of potential destinations, the ease of reaching each destination, and the magnitude, quality, and character of the activities found there" (p. 1175).

When measuring accessibility, scholars tend to follow Geurs and van Wee (2004) who hold that accessibility results from the interaction of the transport system, land-use patterns, and the constraints faced by individuals (Pereira et al., 2019; van Wee & Geurs, 2011). There is an agreement that any measure of accessibility should ideally include elements of the following four components (Geurs & van Wee, 2004). The *land-use component* describes the spatial distribution of activities across the city. The *transportation component* describes the transport system and the time, costs, and effort that individuals must incur to cover a distance between an origin and a destination. The *temporal component* reflects the availability of opportunities at different times of the day, and the time available for individuals to participate in certain activities. Finally, the *individual component* reflects the needs, abilities, and opportunities of individuals to access specific urban resources (Geurs & van Wee, 2004; van Wee & Geurs, 2011).

Recent work has contributed to analytical refinement of the accessibility concept. Levine et al. (2019) hold that accessibility is the outcome of three interacting components: mobility, proximity, and connectivity. Following

Levine et al. (2019), when accessibility is at the top of the hierarchy in urban planning, then mobility, proximity, and connectivity are not ends in themselves but means to achieve the greater goal of increased accessibility. *Mobility* pertains to the realm of transportation planning. An improvement in mobility is usually regarded as "an increase in the territory that can be reached for a given investment of time and money" (Levine et al., 2019, p. 71). *Proximity* belongs to the realm of land-use planning and refers to the spatial distribution of origins and destinations. Land-use policies that increase the number of potential destinations and make them closer to origins contribute to increased accessibility. C*onnectivity*, refers to "the delivery of goods and services to one's location, whether virtually (e.g. internet downloads) or physically (e.g. package delivery, traditional utilities)" (Levine et al., 2019, p. 195). Thus, the key to better understand the underlying factors shaping accessibility is to study the interaction between mobility, proximity, and connectivity. Policies that achieve increases in any each of these factors can result in increased accessibility.

In what follows, I address each of the dimensions of accessibility as proposed by Levine et al. (2019)—proximity, mobility, and connectivity—and further explore their relationship with the mobility experience of workers.

The land-use component of the mobility experience

Urban theorists agree that as an urban economy evolves and grows, the patterns of economic activity across urban space should tend to shift from monocentric to polycentric (Berry & Kim, 1993; Fujita et al., 2001; Kloosterman & Musterd, 2001). To Fujita et al. (2001, as cited in Suárez & Delgado, 2009), the monocentric economy is feasible only until population growth reaches a critical level in which equilibrium is unattainable, and, therefore, it shifts into a non-monocentric economy. Following Kloosterman and Musterd (2001), the monocentric model was the typical construction of industrial 19th-century cities. Nevertheless, as transportation technologies evolved and as cities moved from industrial to service economies, they also shifted from monocentric to polycentric urban forms. Graizbord (2008) provides a useful summary of both types of urban structure:

> *Monocentric urban structure*. A model of a simple mononuclear urban structure in which employment is localized in an urban center and housing is in the periphery. As time goes by, this urban structure is formed by concentric rings which are the outcome of the city's physical and demographic growth.
>
> *Polycentric urban structure*. A model of a complex urban structure that is decentralized, dispersed, and polynuclear. The growth of the city in terms of population and built-up area produces congestion and increases the distance to be traveled in the commute to work. Economic agents (firms) are responsive to this and seek alternative locations for their productive

activities, which results in a supply of jobs outside of the city center and in a spatial system that is decentralized, comprised of several centers.

(Graizbord, 2008: p. 36)

An issue under intense debate is whether the transition toward a polycentric urban form is able to produce a more *efficient* urban system that improves the mobility experience of workers (Bertaud, 2004, 2018; Cervero, 2013; Fuentes, 2008; Suárez & Delgado, 2010). According to Suárez and Delgado (2010), one side of the debate holds that the emergence of new subcenters increases efficiency, as they bring the jobs and services closer to peoples' residential location (Gordon et al., 1986; Levinson & Kumar, 1994). On the other side of the debate, scholars are putting into question the alleged efficiency of polycentrism. Some believe that the new subcenters will attract trips from every corner of the city, which in turn will produce friction due to the increased dispersion between origins and destinations (Bertaud, 2004, 2018; Giuliano & Small, 1993).

Land-use patterns can also operate to increase the distance between workers and jobs, which in the literature is known as the *spatial mismatch hypothesis* (Gobillon et al., 2007; Ihlanfeldt & Sjoquist, 1998; Kain, 1992). According to this hypothesis, the workers who reside in territories with more balanced household-to-jobs ratios are more likely to attain a job than workers in places offering limited job opportunities (Gobillon et al., 2007; Houston, 2005; Hu & Giuliano, 2017; Ihlanfeldt & Sjoquist, 1998; Jin & Paulsen, 2018; Kain, 1968, 1992). The core argument here is that increased spatial accessibility also increases the odds of a person of procuring a job (Hernandez et al., 2020). However, empirical evidence often contradicts the spatial mismatch hypothesis. Research has shown that the high-income population usually reside in neighborhoods with low density of jobs and commute long distances daily (Blumenberg et al., 2015; Ong & Miller, 2005). Therefore, this scholarship contends that transportation within cities should be thought of as an intervening variable in the relationship between jobs and workers, allowing positive outcomes for those with good access to transportation means and negative outcomes for those who lack it.

Cervero (2013) has argued that the spatial mismatch hypothesis, as developed to explain the case of the United States, might unravel in distinct ways in cities of the Global South. According to Cervero (2013), the social geographies within developing cities tend to be much more unequal than those in developed cities. In the words of Cervero,

> (in cities of the Global South) spatial mismatches in where the poor and needy live and where the formal jobs with livable wages are located are more pronounced. In the U.S., the poor often live in older districts just outside the urban core whereas many of the jobs they qualify for are on the periphery. In most of the developing world, the opposite holds: the poor live mainly on the far-flung fringes, isolated from job opportunities

> that are mostly in the urban core. They effectively trade off comparatively high travel costs for cheap housing costs, the opposite of what traditional residential local theory, framed from a first-world perspective, holds.
>
> (2013: p. 13)

Cervero (2013) goes on to highlight how in cities of the Global South the spatial mismatches impose extreme financial burdens on the poor. Research has shown that the trip to work can consume 20 to 25 percent of daily wages in cities of the Global South such as Delhi, Buenos Aires, Mexico City, and Manila, and as high as 30 percent in Nairobi, Pretoria, and Dar es Salaam (Cervero, 2013).

Scholars have traditionally put forward three policy solutions to address the spatial mismatch problem: bringing jobs closer to workers, bringing workers closer to jobs, and better connecting workers to jobs through transit infrastructure (Ihlanfeldt & Sjoquist, 1998). Bringing jobs closer to workers falls in the realm of economic development policy. In free-market capitalist economic systems such as Mexico, it is assumed that firms are free to exercise their location decisions, which in turn shapes the economic geographies of cities. Some authors hold that firms tend to locate near preexisting economic agglomerations as a strategy to optimize economies of agglomeration and localization (Ellison et al., 2010; Sobrino, 2013). Other scholars highlight public investment in productive infrastructure as one of the main factors behind the emergence of new economic agglomerations (Cruz, 2015; Garza, 2013).

Bringing workers closer to jobs falls in the realm of households' residential decisions and housing policy. In the field of accessibility to jobs, there is ample research about how jobs and housing tend to co-locate (Levinson & Kumar, 1994). There are two basic mechanisms through which co-location of jobs and housing can occur (Suárez & Delgado, 2010). The first is that workers choose a residential location as a function of their job location as predicted by the classical location model. In this approach, "households locate as close to the center as their budget allows, at a point where utility is maximized, but where they are outbid by higher-priced economic land uses (Alonso, 1964). As the distance to the center increases, land rent decreases inversely to transport cost" (Suárez et al., 2016: p. 2550). The second mechanism is that workers choose their place of work based on their residential location (Suárez & Delgado, 2010). Research by Levinson and Kumar (1994) showed that, by changing the distributional composition of trip origins and destinations, the co-location of jobs and housing in US metropolitan areas has kept travel times constant, allowing residents to minimize their commute times. However, Suárez et al. (2016) point to research showing that low-income populations have less ability to co-locate as the co-location literature would predict, as the households' ability to co-locate is determined by a series of socioeconomic and spatial variables (Suárez & Delgado, 2010).

Better connecting workers with jobs falls in the realm of mobility and transportation policies, which I discuss in more depth in the next section.

Mobility and public transport

Over the last decade, the field of mobility studies has shifted from a focus on transportation (Graizbord, 2008; Small & Verhoef, 2007)—centered mainly on urban form and movement through roads, flow management, and transit—to an understanding of mobility as a right tied to notions of citizenship (Cresswell, 2006). Following Verlinghieri and Venturini (2018), having access to the city and its resources—including, for example, schools, hospital, and other aspects of cultural, social, and economic life—is inescapably tied to a "getting to" component that is only possible through the fulfillment of the *right to mobility* across urban space. The right to mobility has been defined as

> the right to move in the urban space, to access places and opportunities, but also the right to stay still. . . . The right to mobility subsumes also the right to accessibility, as fundamentally linked to questions of just access to resources and assets.
>
> (Verlinghieri & Venturini, 2018: p. 127)

The ability of cities to provide equitable access to urban resources is important because the right to mobility is closely linked with social mobility. Kaufmann et al. (2004) developed the concept of *motility* to argue that mobility—understood as the spatial distribution of people, goods, and information—is interdependent with social structures. Kaufmann et al. (2004) distinguish between *spatial mobility* defined as "the movement of entities from an origin to a destination along a specific trajectory" (p. 746) and *social mobility* defined as "the transformation in the distribution of resources or social position of individuals, families or groups within a given social structure or network" (p. 747). Based on this distinction, Kaufmann et al. (2004) defined motility as "the capacity of entities (e.g. goods, information or persons) to be mobile in social and geographic space, or as the way in which entities access and appropriate the capacity for socio-spatial mobility according to their circumstances" (p. 750). Thus, to Kaufmann et al. (2004), the main virtue of linking physical and social mobility is "the recognition that movement can take many forms, that different forms of movement may be interchangeable, and that the potentiality of movement can be expressed as a form of movement capital" (p. 752).

Scholars have developed the concepts of *transport disadvantage* (Murray & Davis, 2001), *social disadvantage* (Currie & Delbosc, 2010), and *transport poverty* (Lucas, 2012) for the study of situations in which the lack of accessibility to urban resources produces *social exclusion* (Church et al., 2000; Kenyon et al., 2002; Kenyon, 2003). By *transport disadvantage*, Murray and Davis (2001) refer to the situation in which people in need of public transit services do not have sufficient public transit service opportunities. By *social disadvantage*, Currie and Delbosc (2010) are referring to individuals who are either low-income, unemployed, or have low political engagement, participation, and social support. Lucas (2012) has pointed out that transport disadvantage and social disadvantage are not necessarily synonyms, as research conducted by Currie and Delbosc (2010) showed that "it is possible to be socially excluded but still have good access to transport or to be transport disadvantaged but highly socially included" (Lucas, 2012: p. 106). Rather, transport disadvantage and social disadvantage interact to cause what Lucas (2012) has called *transit poverty*, "which in turn exacerbates the problems of (in)accessibility to opportunities, services and interactions that increase the risk of becoming socially excluded" (Oviedo & Titheridge, 2016: p. 153). Transport-related social exclusion has been defined by Kenyon et al. (2002) as

> the process by which people are prevented from participating in the economic, political and social life of the community because of reduced accessibility to opportunities, services and social networks, due in whole or part to insufficient mobility in a society and environment built around the assumption of high mobility.
>
> (p. 210)

According to Lucas (2012), "it is the high and increasing levels of mobility within the population as a whole that is a key causal factor in the reduced accessibility and, ultimately, exclusion of less mobile sectors of the population" (p. 108). Lastly, Church et al. (2000) identified seven specific features of transport systems that operate to reinforce transport-related social exclusion:

> i) *physical exclusion*: whereby physical barriers, such as vehicle design, lack of disabled facilities or lack of timetable information, inhibit the accessibility of transport services;
> ii) *geographical exclusion*: where a person lives can prevent them from accessing transport services, such as in rural areas or on peripheral urban estates;
> iii) *exclusion from facilities*: the distance of key facilities such as shops, schools, health care or leisure services from where a person lives prevents their access;
> iv) *economic exclusion*: the high monetary costs of travel can prevent or limit access to facilities or employment and thus impact on incomes;
> v) *time-based exclusion*: other demands on time, such as combined work, household and child-care duties, reduces the time available for travel (often referred to as time-poverty in the literature);
> vi) *fear-based exclusion*: where fears for personal safety preclude the use of public spaces and/or transport services;
> vii) *space exclusion*: where security or space management prevent certain groups access to public spaces, e.g. gated communities or first-class waiting rooms at stations.
>
> (as cited in Lucas, 2012: p. 108)

One of the many possible consequences of transit-related social exclusion—and to some extent a strategy used by individuals to cope with such marginalization—is what in the literature has been called the *limited mobility hypothesis* (Calonge, 2018; Faiz, 2011; Lazo & Calderón, 2014). According to this hypothesis, transit-related social exclusion forces the poorest segments of the urban population to limit their search of urban resources to what is most proximate to them. For example, it is argued that the urban poor restrict their travel to essential trips related to work, education, and shopping and "are often confined to walking or at most bicycling, as the weather and topography permits" (Faiz, 2011: p. 40). The limited mobility hypothesis is supported by evidence from studies in cities like Santiago, Chile (Lazo & Calderón, 2014) and Guadalajara, México (Calonge, 2018). In addition to confining the urban poor within their neighborhoods, limited mobility can also be a force that reduces the residential mobility of the urban poor (Lazo & Calderón, 2014). The limited mobility hypothesis is based in the assumption that many individuals face simultaneous and interrelated *transport* and *social disadvantages*.

Connectivity and the mobility experience

In the framework proposed by Levine et al. (2019), *connectivity* refers specifically to "the delivery of goods and services to one's location, whether virtually (e.g. internet downloads) or physically (e.g. package delivery, traditional utilities)" (p. 195). This understanding of connectivity might be a suitable one for a wide array of resources provided by cities. However, when applied to job accessibility, the connectivity dimension as thought of by Levine et al. (2019) has to be enhanced to include connectivity to labor markets. When labor markets in an urban region are highly segmented (Bowles et al., 2018), being *connected* to labor markets that provide job security becomes of paramount importance. According to Bowles et al. (2018),

> labor markets are described as segmented – that is, divided into separate, or distinct, markets – when the demanders and suppliers of labor in one market do not compete with demanders with suppliers in other markets. Instead of having one large market for all jobs and all workers, there are, in effect, different market "segments" – each with its own demand for labor (by employers) and supply for labor (by workers). Labor markets may be segmented either because workers in some jobs are shielded from competition with other workers or because workers are excluded from competing for certain jobs.
>
> (pp. 152–153)

There are several mechanisms through which labor markets can become and remain segmented (Bowles et al., 2018). The development of unions and labor accords between unions and employers can shield workers from wider competition. Large firms can impose bureaucratic control, organizing their labor process by stratifying their workforce, establishing job ladders, and awarding seniority-based promotions according to explicit rules. Job discrimination is another cause of the segmented labor market, as it prevents workers with specific socioeconomic characteristics from competing for specific jobs.

Following Bowles et al. (2018), the interplay of labor accords, bureaucratic control, and job discrimination has produced three relatively distinct labor markets: the *independent primary labor market* includes those bureaucratically organized jobs that offer stable employment, often with considerable job security, clearly defined career paths, and relatively high pay (e.g., technicians, scientists, supervisors, and managers, etc.); the *subordinate primary labor market* includes most government employment as well as the jobs of the traditional unionized industrial working class (e.g., autoworkers, truckers, steelworkers, etc.); while the *secondary market* includes most of the remaining workers in dead-end jobs who have few protections from economy-wide labor market competition (e.g., nonunion factories, nonunion janitors, waitresses, guards, etc.) (Bowles et al., 2018: pp. 153–155).

Circling back to the accessibility literature, Geurs and van Wee (2004) have called on accessibility scholars to put special attention on individuals' characteristics in the determination of accessibility outcomes. According to Geurs and van Wee (2004), the age, educational level, household situation, travel budget, skills, and physical conditions of people may strongly influence the kind of jobs that people qualify for and therefore affect the total aggregate accessibility result. Suárez et al. (2016) point out to research suggesting the existence of "dual cities," "where unequal access to education makes high-skilled jobs unobtainable to low-wage workers, who are then left behind in dead-end jobs in the informal sector" (p. 2551).

When the framework developed by Levine et al. (2019) is applied to the case of accessibility to jobs, there is a potential tension between the *proximity* and *connectivity* dimensions. The tension arises from the interaction between the spatial location of the demand for labor and the residential location of workers. On one hand, policies that shift the demand for labor to territories further away from the residential location of workers may produce decreased proximity. On the other hand, when education policies increase workers' access to primary labor markets that are located further away from their residential locations, connectivity may be increased but proximity is decreased. This means that increased connectivity may come at the expense of decreased proximity. As these examples convey, an increase in connectivity that produces a decrease in proximity can operate to decrease overall accessibility.

Urban political economy

The field of urban political economy examines how urban development shapes and is shaped by the decisions and activities of economic, social, and governmental actors (Nevarez, 2015). Urban political economy assumes that "the city's form, economy, and political structures comprise a dynamic, contradictory mechanism for the appropriation of wealth" (Nevarez, 2015, p. 1). Thus, from the lens of urban political economy, urban-related public policies can be understood as the output of negotiation and compromise between economic, social, and governmental actors whose interests overlap in urban space. The PIF builds on two theories developed by urban political economy scholars: the theory of the city as a colossal productive force (Garza, 2013, 2014, 2015) and the literature on the urban commons (Chatterton, 2010; Harvey, 2013; Kip, 2015).

Over the last four decades, Professor Gustavo Garza from El Colegio de México has worked on integrating several streams of classical political economy and neo-Marxian literatures to ensemble a comprehensive theory of the city as a productive force (Garza, 1980, 2013, 2020). According to this theory, urban regions are the material basis that enables and makes the capitalist economic system possible. This is so because urban areas are constituted by layers of infrastructures that allow the flow of production and consumption and, as the world continues to urbanize at a fast rate, most of economic activity today takes place in cities. Firms can provide the infrastructure that is within their reach. But historically, it has been the role of the state to provide the major productive infrastructures whose investment would be so large that no single firm would ever be able to provide (List, 1841; Marx, 1867; Smith, 1776). Accordingly, Professor Garza argues that urban areas are composed of two kinds of state-provided infrastructures: socialized means of production (Folin, 1981; Pianta, 1989) and means of collective consumption (Castells, 1977, 1983).

The *socialized means of production* include state-provided infrastructures such as roads, highways, airports, pipelines, damns, electric plants, and so on, that support productive processes (Garza, 2013). The kinds of socialized means of production that ought to be provided by the state are influenced by and evolve with the kind of goods and services that are produced in an urban economy. This means that the built environment of cities must be constantly shaped and reshaped to provide the infrastructures that are needed by the ever-shifting productive processes (López-García, 2022). The *means of collective consumption* are the state-provided infrastructures—such as public housing, schools, public parks, transportation, and so on—that help in the reproduction of the labor force and to dampen class conflict, which is essential for the maintenance of the capitalist economic system (Hall, 2014). Governments north and south intervene in the consumption processes by providing collective goods and services (Castells, 1977, 1983), which in turn is one of the most formative elements in the making and remaking of urban space (Katznelson, 1992). Together, the *socialized means of production* and the *means of collective consumption* constitute the city as a colossal productive force (Garza, 2013).

Within this infrastructural context, there is intense dispute between economic, social, and governmental actors about the extent to which the means of collective consumption in an urban region should remain an urban common or if they should be commodified. Influential urban scholars such as Harvey (2003) and Graham and Marvin (2001) have shed light on how present-day processes of commodification and privatization of urban services are a key mechanism through which urban actors achieve to appropriate of urban wealth. As a response to this trend, scholars and activists have advanced the concept of the *urban commons* as a gateway to the politics of de-commodifying urban life (Chatterton, 2010; Harvey, 2013; Kip, 2015). Following Nikolaeva et al. (2019), the notion of the urban commons has been primarily engaged through two academic discussions. The first relates to the management of common pool resources beyond the state and the market. This discussion remains focused on infrastructure management aiming to increase the provision of urban public goods and common pool resources (Frischmann, 2012). The second discussion calls to look beyond the simple physical attributes of infrastructures and see the "commons as complex social and political ecologies which articulate particular socio-spatial practices, social relationships, and forms of governance that underpin them to produce and reproduce them" (Chatterton, 2010, p. 626). The urban commons, then, are made real through political engagement and the practice of *commoning* (Chatterton, 2010; Huron, 2015).

Additionally, urban political economy provides lens for the empirical investigation of how urban change is influenced by the actions of specific urban actors who have their own agenda and capacity to shape public policy (Verduzco, 2013, 2021). Urban change does not take place within an unstoppable structural process. Instead, the production of specific accessibility outcomes can be conceptualized as the product of the interaction within a fragmented elite of urban actors, and most importantly, of an asymmetry of power between elite actors and workers (Verduzco, 2013). In this sense, urban political economy can support this investigation by enabling a closer look at the activities of key urban actors shaping the policy decisions affecting accessibility outcomes.

Policy feedback theory

Policy feedback theory (Mettler & Sorelle, 2017) holds that policies, once operating, restructure subsequent political processes by becoming an additional layer to the institutional setting within which policymaking takes place (Mettler, 2016; Mettler & Sorelle, 2017; Skocpol, 1992). The theory holds that policies have *feedback effects* that can reshape the attitudes and behavior of actors within a policy subsystem and affect the evolution of policymaking institutions and interest groups. Once institutionalized, every new policy adds an additional layer to the thousands of norms, rules, and practices navigated by policy professionals, interest groups, and clienteles (Lascoumes & Le Galès, 2014). In this way, policies enacted in time A can affect the policy process and the kinds of policies that are feasible in time B (Mettler & Soss, 2004; Pierson, 1993).

According to Mettler and Sorelle (2017), scholars in the field of policy feedback have focused on examining four major streams of policy feedback inquiry. First, policies in time A can affect *political agendas* and the *definition of policy problems* in time B. Policies created in earlier points can affect which problems are worthy of public attention and government action, and how such problems are understood and defined. Second, policies in time A might affect the *forms of governance* that are feasible in time B. Once established, policies may shape the policy alternatives available to policymakers, the type of institutional arrangements assigned to new policies, and even the parameters of government action. Third, policies in time A may influence the *power of groups* in time B. As public policies provide resources and have distributive effects, policies themselves can shape which kinds of groups will form and grow and which will fail to coalesce. Fourth, policies in time A may affect the *meaning of citizenship* in time B, defined broadly as "the rights, duties, and obligations imposed by governments as well as citizens' responses to them, including their political attitudes and participation" (Mettler & Sorelle, 2017: p. 113).

In addition to the previously mentioned streams of inquiry, scholars in the field of policy feedback theory have proposed two feedback mechanisms through which policies in time A produce a variety of effects over policy processes in time B: *resources effects* and *interpretive effects* (Mettler & Sorelle, 2017). *Resources effects* refer to the ability of policies to distribute resources among actors. Many public policies offer citizens payments, goods, or services. Other policies take resources away from citizens, like in the case of collecting taxes or imposing fines. The distributional effects of policies may increase political participation by providing individuals and organizations with incentives to mobilize and advocate in their defense. Public policies also impose rules and procedures on citizens that may be the source of interpretive effects, also called "cognitive" or "learning effects." *Interpretive effects* refer to the ability of public policies to shape norms, values, and attitudes, which can be fostered through the impact of resources or directly through features of policy design and implementation (Mettler & Sorelle, 2017). Interpretive effects convey messages to people about the government and their relationship to it, and the status of other citizens, which, in turn, will shape subsequent political engagement.

The Policy Interactions Framework (PIF)

The Policy Interactions Framework (PIF) is designed to step out of the traditional domains approach. The goal is to provide an analytical framework for the investigation of the long-term interactions between policies from distinct policy domains in the production of urban outcomes. The PIF is based on three assumptions. First, urban outcomes are the result of the interactions between policies from different policy domains, rather than the result of policies from a single policy silo. Second, public policies are inevitably embedded within the urban political economy of the cities in which they are deployed. That is, public policies shape and are shaped by the decisions and activity of economic and political actors seeking the appropriation of urban wealth. And third, the political economy within a policy domain can sometimes produce outputs that become inputs in the policy processes within a distinct policy domain.

The PIF is presented in Figure 2.1. Applying the PIF consists of a series of steps that are taken in distinct phases of a research project. The PIF begins in the research design phase by selecting the policy domains that will be traced and investigated (panel a). The selection of the policy domains must be based on a literature review about the issue under study. There is no limit on the

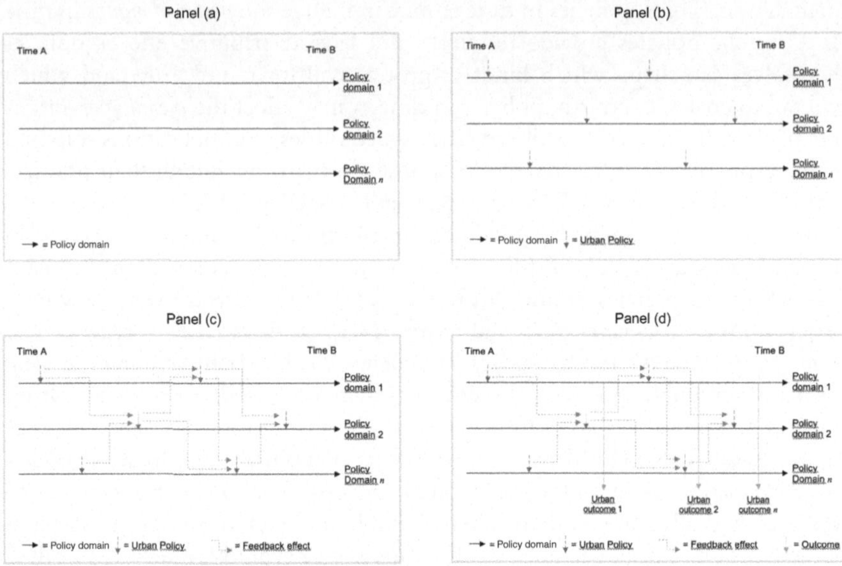

Figure 2.1 The Policy Interactions Framework

number of policy domains that could be traced, but the analyst must consider that increasing the number of policy domains will proportionally complicate the empirical research. Then, a period for the analysis must be selected. In panel a, the time frame for the study is depicted as the period between time A and time B. The PIF is designed for the study of long-term policy interactions. For that reason, the time frame should not be too short.

The next step in the PIF is to identify the specific policies in each policy domain likely to be interacting to produce specific urban outcomes (panel b). Identifying such policies is not a simple task. Sometimes, the policy analyst has previous knowledge about the urban outcome under study and can select the policies to be analyzed *a priori*. In this case, the selection of the policies under study can be done during the research design phase. However, when such *a priori* knowledge is not at hand, the analyst can resort to a couple of empirical strategies. Sometimes, preliminary research can point out to the urban policies that ought to be included in the study. Other times, the urban policies to be included must be identified during the data collection phase of the research project.

The fourth step of the framework consists of identifying and characterizing relevant feedback effects between policy domains (panel c). This step can only be done during the data collection phase. Regardless of the data collection method being used, the analyst should make sure that the data collection instruments include the analytical categories proposed by the PIF. The purpose of the analysis is to identify specific urban policy outputs within a policy domain that then become inputs in the policy process of a distinct policy area. The last step of the framework takes place during the data analysis phase (panel d). The data collected should be analyzed aiming to identify the ways in which urban policies from distinct policy domains have interacted to produce specific urban outcomes across the period under study. As such period can be long, it is possible to identify several urban outcomes in different points in time.

The following chapters present a series of empirical studies that will be then analyzed through the PIF. Chapter 3 conducts an empirical study of time and distance in the journey to work in MCMZ to assess the spatial distribution of inequalities in the mobility situations of workers. Chapter 4 investigates shifts in the spatial location of the demand for labor. Chapter 5 investigates the role of housing policy in increasing the physical separation between workers and jobs. Chapter 6 presents a study of how public transport policies have contributed to the commodification of public transport services. Finally, Chapter 7 applies the PIF to produce a unifying assessment of the findings from Chapters 3, 4, 5, and 6.

References

Alonso, W. (1964). *Location and land use: Toward a general theory of land rent*. Cambridge: Harvard University Press.

Bazurli, R. (2020). How urban is urban policy making? *PS – Political Science and Politics*, *53*(1), 25–28.

Berry, B. J. L., & Kim, H. -M. (1993). Challenges to the monocentric model. *Geographical Analysis*, *25*(1), 1–4.

Bertaud, A. (2004). *The spatial organization of cities: Deliberate outcome or unforeseen consequence?* (Working Paper 2004–01). Institute of Urban and Regional Development. Berkeley: University of California Berkeley.

Bertaud, A. (2018). *Order without design: How markets shape cities*. Cambridge: MIT Press.

Blumenberg, E., Pierce, G., & Smart, M. (2015). Transportation access, residential location, and economic opportunity: Evidence from two housing voucher experiments. *Cityscape: A Journal of Policy Development and Research*, *17*(2), 89–111.

Bowles, S., Edwards, R., Frank, R., & Mehrene, L. (2018). *Understanding capitalism: Competition, command, and change*. Oxford: Oxford University Press.

Calonge, F. (2018). Recursos de movilidad y accesibiidad urbana en los municipios del sur del Área Metropolitana de Guadalajara, México. *Revista Urbano*, *38*, 48–57.

Castells, M. (1977). *The urban question*. Cambridge: MIT Press.

Castells, M. (1983). *The city and the grassroots: A cross-cultural theory of urban social movements*. Berkeley and Los Angeles: University of California Press.

Cervero, R. (2013). Linking urban transport and land use in developing countries. *Journal of Transport and Land Use*, *6*(1), 7–24.

Chatterton, P. (2010). Seeking the urban common: Furthering the debate on spatial justice. *City*, *14*(6), 625–628.

Church, A., Frost, M., & Sullivan, K. (2000). Transport and social exclusion in London. *Transport Policy*, 7, 195–205.

Cohen, M. A. (2016). From Habitat II to Pachamama: A growing agenda and diminishing expectations for Habitat III. *Environment and Urbanization, 28*(1), 35–48.
Crawford, M. (2018). Abandoning silos: How innovative governments are collaborating horizontally to solve complex problems. *Mowat Centre*. Toronto: University of Toronto.
Cresswell, T. (2006). The right to mobility: The production of mobility in the courtroom. *Antipode, 38*(4), 735–754.
Cruz, F. (2015). *Configuración espacial de la industria en la Ciudad de México*. Ciudad de México: El Colegio de México.
Cui, B., Boisjoly, G., El-Geneidy, A., & Levinson, D. (2019). Accessibility and the journey to work through the lens of equity. *Journal of Transport Geography, 74*, 269–277.
Currie, G., & Delbosc, A. (2010). Modelling the social and psychological impacts of transport disadvantage. *Transportation, 37*(6), 953–966.
Duranton, G., & Guerra, E. (2016). Developing a common narrative on urban accessibility: An urban planning perspective. In *Brookings: Moving to access*. Washington, D.C.: The Brookings Institution.
Ellison, G., Glaeser, E. L., & Kerr, W. R. (2010). What causes industry agglomeration? Evidence from coagglomeration patterns. *American Economic Review, 100*(3), 1195–1213.
Faiz, A. (2011). Transportation and the urban poor. *ITE Journal (Institute of Transportation Engineers), 81*(12), 40–43.
Folin, M. (1981). The production of the general conditions of social reproduction and the role of the state. In M. Harloe & E. Lebas (Eds.), *City, class, and capital: New developments in the political economy of cities and regions*. London: Arnold.
Frischmann, B. M. (2012). *Infrastructure: The social value of shared resources*. Oxford: Oxford University Press.
Fuentes, C. M. (2008). La estructura urbana y las diferencias espaciales en el tiempo de traslado del viaje al trabajo en Ciudad Juárez, Chihuahua. *Estudios Demográficos y Urbanos, 23*(1), 55–81.
Fujita, M., Krugman, P., & Venables, A. J. (2001). *The spatial economy*. Cambridge: MIT Press.
Garza, G. (1980). Modo de producción y urbanización (bosquejo preliminar). *Demografía y Economía, 14*(1), 68–89.
Garza, G. (2013). *Teoría de las condiciones y los servicios generales de la producción*. Ciudad de México: El Colegio de México.
Garza, G. (2014). *Valor de los medios de producción socializados en la Ciudad de México*. Ciudad de México: El Colegio de México.
Garza, G. (2015). *Valor de los medios de consumo colectivo en la Ciudad de México*. Ciudad de México: El Colegio de México.
Garza, G. (2020). *Economía política de la estructuración del comercio y los servicios en la Ciudad de México*. Ciudad de México: ePromethium Ediciones Digitales.
Geurs, K. T., & van Wee, B. (2004). Accessibility evaluation of land-use and transport strategies: Review and research directions. *Journal of Transport Geography, 12*(2), 127–140.
Giuliano, G., & Small, K. A. (1993). Is the journey to work explained by urban structure? *Urban Studies, 30*(9), 1485–1500.
Gobillon, L., Selod, H., & Zenou, Y. (2007). The mechanisms of spatial mismatch. *Urban Studies, 44*(12), 2401–2428.
Gordon, P., Richardson, H., & Wong, H. (1986). The distribution of population and employment in a polycentric city: The case of Los Angeles. *Environment and Planning A, 18*(2), 161–173.

Graham, S., & Marvin, S. (2001). *Splintering urbanism: Networked infrastructures, technological mobilities and the urban condition*. London: Routledge.

Graizbord, B. (2008). *Geografía del transporte público en el área metropolitana de la Ciudad de México*. Ciudad de México: El Colegio de México.

Hall, P. (2014). *Cities of tomorrow: An intellectual history of urban planning and design since 1880*. Hoboken: Wiley-Blackwell.

Handy, S. L., & Niemeier, D. A. (1997). Measuring accessibility: An exploration of issues and alternatives. *Environment and Planning A, 29*, 1175–1194.

Harvey, D. (2003). *The new imperialism*. Oxford: Oxford University Press.

Harvey, D. (2013). *Rebel cities: From the right to the city to the urban revolution*. London and New York: Verso.

Hernandez, D., Hansz, M., & Massobrio, R. (2020). Job accessibility through public transport and unemployment in Latin America: The case of Montevideo (Uruguay). *Journal of Transport Geography, 85*, 102742.

Houston, D. S. (2005). Methods to test the spatial mismatch hypothesis. *Economic Geography, 81*(4), 407–434.

Hu, L., & Giuliano, G. (2017). Poverty concentration, job access, and employment outcomes. *Journal of Urban Affairs, 39*(1), 1–16.

Huron, A. (2015). Working with strangers in saturated space: Reclaiming and maintaining the urban commons. *Antipode, 47*(4), 963–979.

Ihlanfeldt, K. R., & Sjoquist, D. L. (1998). The spatial mismatch hypothesis: A review of recent studies and their implications for welfare reform. *Housing Policy Debate, 9*(4), 849–892.

Jin, J., & Paulsen, K. (2018). Does accessibility matter? Understanding the effect of job accessibility on labour market outcomes. *Urban Studies, 55*(1), 91–115.

Kain, J. F. (1968). Housing segregation, negro employment, and metropolitan decentralization. *The Quarterly Journal of Economics, 82*(2), 175–197.

Kain, J. F. (1992). The spatial mismatch hypothesis: Three decades later. *Housing Policy Debate, 3*(2), 371–460.

Katznelson, I. (1992). *Marxism and the city*. Oxford: Oxford University Press.

Kaufmann, V., Bergman, M. M., & Joye, D. (2004). Motility: Mobility as capital. *International Journal of Urban and Regional Research, 28*(4), 745–756.

Kellerman, A. (2006). *Personal mobilities*. New York and London: Routledge.

Kenyon, S. (2003). Understanding social exclusion and social inclusion. *Municipal Engineer, 156*(ME2), 97–104.

Kenyon, S., Lyons, G., & Rafferty, J. (2002). Transport and social exclusion: Investigating the possibility of promoting inclusion through virtual mobility. *Journal of Transport Geography, 10*, 207–219.

Kip, M. (2015). Moving beyond the city: Conceptualizing urban commons from a critical urban studies perspective. In M. Dellenbaugh, M. Kip, M. Bieniok, A. Müller, & M. Schwegmann (Eds.), *Urban commons: Moving beyond state and market*. Basel: Birkhäuser.

Kloosterman, R. C., & Musterd, S. (2001). The polycentric urban region: Towards a research agenda. *Urban Studies, 38*(4), 623–633.

Lascoumes, P., & Le Galès, P. (2014). *Sociología de la acción pública*. Ciudad de México: El Colegio de México.

Lazo, A., & Calderón, R. (2014). Los anclajes en la proximidad y la movilidad cotidiana. Retrato de tres barrios de la ciudad de Santiago de Chile. *Eure, 40*(121), 207–226.

Levine, J., Grengs, J., & Merlin, L. A. (2019). *From mobility to accessibility: Transforming urban transportation and land-use planning*. Ithaca: Cornell University Press.

Levinson, D., & Kumar, A. (1994). The rational locator: Why travel times have remained stable. *Journal of the American Planning Association, 60*(3), 319–332.

List, F. (1841). The national system of political economy. Pantianos Classics.

López-García, D. (2022). Building inequality: Infrastructure and intra-urban inequality in the capitalist city. In D. Iossifova, A. Gasparatos, S. Zavos, Y. Gamal, & Y. Long (Eds.), *Urban Infrastructuring: Reconfigurations, transformations and sustainability in the Global South*. Singapore: Springer Nature.

Lucas, K. (2012). Transport and social exclusion: Where are we now? *Transport Policy, 20*, 105–113.

Marx, K. (1867). *Capital. Volume I*. London: Penguin Classics.

McCann, E. J. (2008). Expertise, truth, and urban policy mobilities: Global circuits of knowledge in the development of Vancouver, Canada's "four pillar" drug strategy. *Environment and Planning A, 40*(4), 885–904.

Mettler, S. (2016). The policyscape and the challenges of contemporary politics to policy maintenance. *Perspectives on Politics, 14*(2), 369–390.

Mettler, S., & Sorelle, M. (2017). Policy feedback theory. In C. M. Weible & P. Sabatie (Eds.), *Theories of the Policy Process (4th ed.)*. New York and London: Routledge.

Mettler, S., & Soss, J. (2004). The consequences of public policy for democratic citizenship: Bridging policy studies and mass politics. *Perspectives on Politics, 2*(1), 55–73.

Murray, A. T., & Davis, R. (2001). Equity in regional service provision. *Journal of Regional Science, 41*(4), 577–600.

Nevarez, L. (2015). Urban political economy. In *The Blackwell Encyclopedia of Sociology*. Hoboken, NJ: John Wiley & Sons, Ltd.

Nikolaeva, A., Adey, P., Cresswell, T., Lee, J. Y., Nóvoa, A., & Temenos, C. (2019). Commoning mobility: Towards a new politics of mobility transitions. *Transactions of the Institute of British Geographers, 44*, 346–360.

Ong, P., & Miller, D. (2005). Spatial and transportation mismatch in Los Angeles. *Journal of Planning Education and Research, 25*(1), 43–56.

Oviedo, D., & Titheridge, H. (2016). Mobilities of the periphery: Informality, access and social exclusion in the urban fringe in Colombia. *Journal of Transport Geography, 55*, 152–164.

Páez, A., Scott, D. M., & Morency, C. (2012). Measuring accessibility: Positive and normative implementations of various accessibility indicators. *Journal of Transport Geography, 25*, 141–153.

Pereira, R. H. M., Banister, D., Schwanen, T., & Wessel, N. (2019). Distributional effects of transport policies on inequalities in access to opportunities in Rio de Janeiro. *Journal of Transport and Land Use, 12*(1), 741–764.

Pianta, M. (1989). The conditions of production: A note. *Capitalism Nature Socialism, 1*(3), 129–134.

Pierson, P. (1993). When effect becomes cause: Policy feedback and political change. *World Politics, 45*(4), 595–628.

Robinson, J. (2015). "Arriving at" urban policies: The topological spaces of urban policy mobility. *International Journal of Urban and Regional Research, 39*(4), 831–834.

Skocpol, T. (1992). *Protecting soldiers and mothers: The political origins of social policy in the United States*. Cambridge: Belkman Press of Harvard University Press.

Small, K., & Verhoef, E. (2007). *The economics of urban transportation*. London and New York: Routledge.

Smith, A. (1776). *An inquiry into the nature and causes of the wealth of nations. Volume II*. Indianapolis: Liberty Fund.

Sobrino, J. (2013). Infraestructura, economías de aglomeración y competitividad urbana. In G. Garza (Ed.), *Teoría de las Condiciones y los Servivcios Generales de la Producción*. Ciudad de México: El Colegio de México.

Suárez, M., & Delgado, J. (2009). Is Mexico City polycentric? A trip attaction capacity approach. *Urban Studies*, *46*(10), 2187–2211.

Suárez, M., & Delgado, J. (2010). Patrones de movilidad residencial en la ciudad de México como evidencia de co-localización de población y empleos. *Eure*, *36*(107), 67–71.

Suárez, M., Murata, M., & Delgado Campos, J. (2016). Why do the poor travel less? Urban structure, commuting and economic informality in Mexico City. *Urban Studies*, *53*(12), 2548–2566.

van Wee, B., & Geurs, K. T. (2011). Discussing equity and social exclusion in accessibility evaluations. *European Journal of Transport and Infrastructure Research*, *11*(4), 350–367.

Verduzco, B. (2013). *Una utopía urbana (im)posible. La negociación infinita de planes de desarrollo urbano y prosperidad*. Guadalajara: Universidad de Guadalajara.

Verduzco, B. (2021). *Extraterrenal: Cómo hacerse de una casa con o sin ayuda del gobierno*. Guadalajara: Academia Jaliscience de Ciencias, A.C.

Verlinghieri, E., & Venturini, F. (2018). Exploring the right to mobility through the 2013 mobilizations in Rio de Janeiro. *Journal of Transport Geography*, *67*, 126–136.

3 Diverging mobility situations of workers in Greater Mexico City

The study of the journey to work is telling of broader intra-urban socioeconomic inequalities within urban regions. In Latin American cities, the land values of areas closer to job-rich zones tend to be higher while values in peripheral areas further away from job concentrations are usually lower. This spatial distribution of land values operates to sort the residential location of workers throughout urban space according to their income. Workers with the higher-paying jobs, which are usually located within existing employment subcenters, can afford to live closer to their jobs. Low-earning workers, on the other hand, must retreat into the affordable housing stock that is usually located further away from employment concentrations. As a result, the cost that workers must pay in terms of commuting time and distance tends to be lower for high-income workers and higher for low-income workers.

A study of the policy interactions that have shaped inequalities in the journey to work must begin by taking stock of the scope and spatial distribution of such. This chapter serves this purpose and sets the stage for the empirical studies presented later in this book on the location of jobs (Chapter 4), housing pathways (Chapter 5), and public transport (Chapter 6). Understanding inequalities in time and distance in the journey to work is important because the commuting experience of workers has an important effect on their overall well-being. Research shows that a longer commute can reduce workers' overall happiness (Kahneman et al., 2004) because it is associated with lower job and leisure time satisfaction and with poor mental health (Clark et al., 2020).

By analyzing a subsample of the journey to work from the Mexico City Metropolitan Zone (MCMZ) 2017 Origin-Destination Household Survey, I calculate average time and distance in the journey to work for 194 travel districts in MCMZ. Then, following the methodology proposed by Niedzielski and Boschmann (2014), I classify travel districts into one of four categories of mobility situations: Short Commutes, Long Commutes, Wormholes, or Transit Hells. I assume that workers living in Short Commute and Wormhole travel districts have a better mobility situation than workers living in Long Commutes and Transit Hells. The results of the study demonstrate that the spatial distribution of mobility situations in MCMZ shows a concentric pattern, with most Short Commute districts located toward the central and western areas of the metropolitan region, while Transit Hells form

DOI: 10.4324/9781003261698-3

a belt that encloses the Short Commute districts. Peripheral areas are composed of a combination of Long Commutes and Wormholes. Eastern-MCMZ, the book's case study, has some of the highest commuting time and distance across the urban region and is mostly composed of Long Commute districts.

The chapter is organized as follows. I begin by presenting the analytical strategy for the study, the data, and methods used. I then present the results of the study. An analysis of the distribution of time and distance by percentiles allows the calculation of a 90/10 ratio, which shows the scope of inequalities in the mobility situations of workers. An ANOVA analysis is then presented, which tests for significant differences in commuting time and distance between the categories of mobility situations. Finally, I present maps of commuting time (Map 3.1), distance (Map 3.2), and the categories of mobility situations (Map 3.3), which show the spatial distribution of inequalities in the mobility situations of workers in Greater Mexico City.

Analytical strategy and research methods

The efforts to measure accessibility to jobs are far from settled in the literature (Geurs & van Wee, 2004; Páez et al., 2012; van Wee & Geurs, 2011). Traditional metrics of accessibility to jobs assume that it takes less time to cover shorter distances and that it is easier to travel between more proximate than less proximate locations (Bocarejo & Oviedo, 2012; Grengs, 2012; Handy & Niemeier, 1997). However, recent critique by Niedzielski and Boschmann (2014) has shown that depending on the socioeconomic characteristics of workers, the land-use patterns across an urban region, and available transportation networks, this assumption might not always hold. In this case, the relationship between commuting distance and time could become inverted—particular people in particular locations might experience longer or shorter travel times than expected for a given travel distance. This gives room to what Niedzielski and Boschmann call *diverging mobility situations*, that is, the experience of reaching jobs "could be different for different people originating from the same location" (Niedzielski & Boschmann, 2014, p. 1163).

This study investigates diverging mobility situations in MCMZ based on the methodology proposed by Niedzielski and Boschmann (2014). In their study of the Denver Metropolitan Statistical Area, Niedzielski and Boschmann (2014) analyzed travel time and distance for workers in a sample of 619 census tracts. The authors assigned each census tract to one of four categories based on whether that tract's travel time and distance fell above or below the average among all 619 tracts. A summary of the categories is provided in Figure 3.1. The tracts with above-average travel time and above-average distance (upper right) are classified as *Long Commutes*. The tracts with below-average travel time and below-average distance (bottom left) are classified as *Short Commutes*. These two categories represent the two expected Cartesian commuting experience categories; that is, expected proximities of long commutes and short commutes. In contrast, the next two categories represent inverted and unexpected proximities. Tracts with below-average travel time but above-average distance (bottom right) are classified as

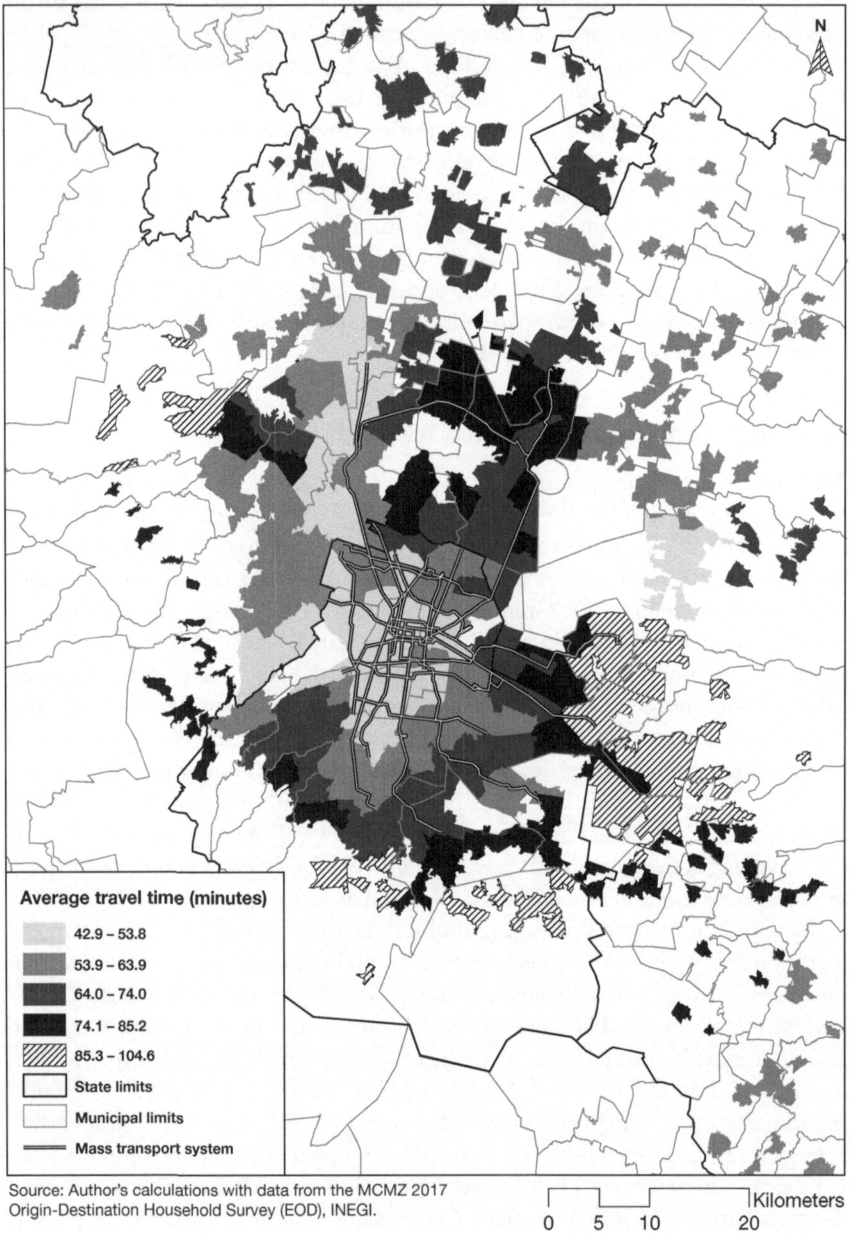

Map 3.1 Average time in the journey to work, MCMZ, 2017

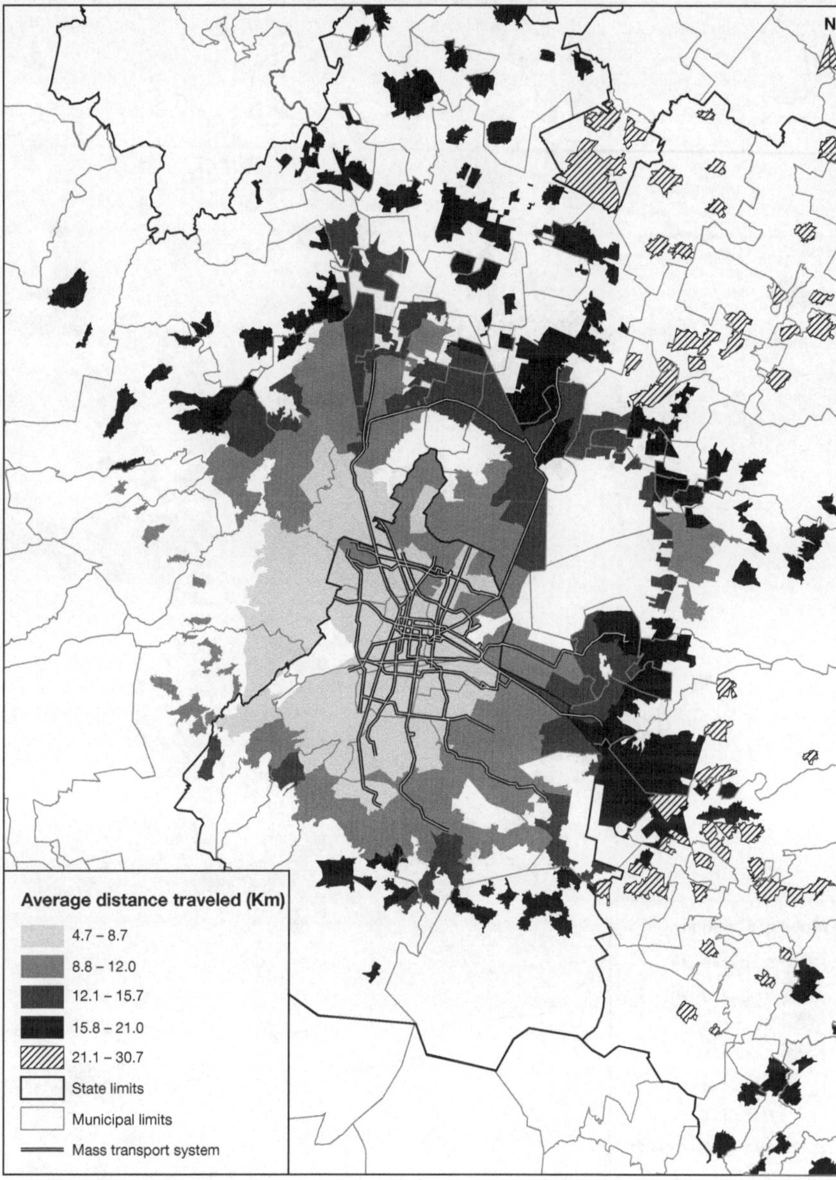

Source: Author's calculations with data from the MCMZ 2017 Origin-Destination Household Survey (EOD), INEGI.

Map 3.2 Average distance in the journey to work, MCMZ, 2017

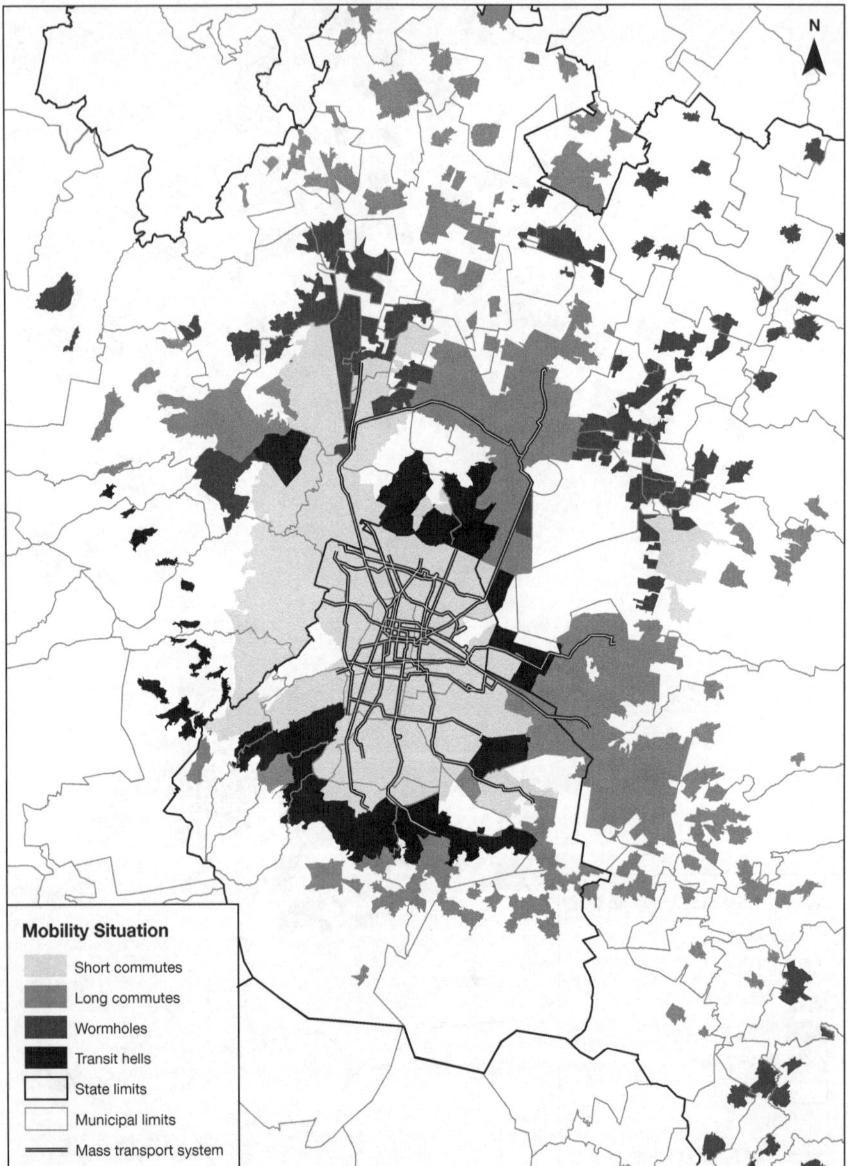

Source: Author's calculations with data from the MCMZ 2017 Origin-Destination Household Survey (EOD), INEGI.

Map 3.3 Diverging mobility situations in MCMZ, 2017

		Average distance to jobs	
		Below	Above
Average travel time to jobs	Above	Transit Hell (unexpected)	Long commute (expected)
	Below	Short commute (expected)	Wormholes (unexpected)

Figure 3.1 Adapted from Niedzielski and Boschmann's (2014) positionality categories

Wormholes, while tracts with above-average travel time but below-average distance (upper left) are classified as *Transit Hells*.

The study is based on calculating average time and distance in the journey to work to classify MCMZ into the mobility situations proposed by Niedzielski and Boschmann (2014). The data are taken from the MCMZ Origin-Destination Household Survey (EOD-2017) developed in 2017 by the National Institute of Statistics, Geography and Informatics (INEGI, by its acronym in Spanish). The EOD-2017 is representative at the travel district level, which is greater than a census tract but smaller than a municipality. In the EOD-2017, the MCMZ is divided into 194 travel districts: 85 are in Mexico City, 108 in the State of Mexico, and one in the state of Hidalgo.[1] The EOD-2017 provides information for a sample of 531,594 trips.

A subsample of the journey to work is taken for this study, which selected the trips of the EOD-2017 with the following characteristics: (i) trips whose origin is the home of respondents, (ii) trips whose purpose is reaching the workplace, (iii) trips made during a weekday, and (iv) trips made through any of the MCMZ public transport systems.[2] The trips that involved the use of a private vehicle, were made only by bicycle or walking, or whose destination was a workplace outside of the MCMZ were removed from the subsample. After selecting the trips with the previously mentioned characteristics, the subsample for the study is composed of 39,655 trips. The subsample is still representative at the travel district level, as the average sample for each district is 205 trips, with the number of cases ranging from 59 to 327.[3]

It would have been ideal to create several subsamples of trips to work, one per main transport mode such as public transport and private vehicle. There is enough evidence in the literature that a private vehicle increases the distance traveled during the journey to work, therefore providing access to labor markets located at a larger distance from people's homes (Blumenberg et al., 2015; Ong & Miller, 2005; Shen, 1998). However, when trying to extract a subsample of the journey to work by private vehicle from the EOD-2017, many of the travel districts resulted in a sample of fewer than 50 cases. This would have compromised the representativeness of the study. Therefore, only the subsample of trips to work through public transport is analyzed.

The methodology to classify travel districts into a mobility situation category consists of the following steps. First, I extracted the total number of trips for all pairs of district-to-district combinations with observed flows. Second, for each travel district pair, the median[4] travel time in minutes was calculated. Third, I computed the average travel time for each travel district weighting by the number of trips in each combination of district-to-district pair.[5] Replicating the methodology proposed by Niedzielski and Boschmann (2014), the commuting flow weighted travel time is calculated through the following formula,

$$\bar{T}_i = \frac{\sum_{ij} P_{ij} \times t_{ij}}{\sum_{ij} P_{ij}}$$

and the commute flow weighted distance is calculated as follows,

$$\bar{D}_i = \frac{\sum_{ij} P_{ij} \times d_{ij}}{\sum_{ij} P_{ij}}$$

where:

T_i = commute weighted average travel time for travel district i.
D_i = commute weighted average distance for travel district i.
i = origin travel district (home location), $i = 1, \ldots, n$.
j = destination travel district (job location), $j = 1, \ldots, n$.
t_{ij} = travel time between home i and job j.
d_{ij} = distance between home i and job j.
P_i = number of workers commuting from home i to job j.

Finally, I followed the steps used by Niedzielski and Boschmann (2014) and assigned each travel district to one of four positionality categories: Short Commutes, Long Commutes, Wormholes, and Transit Hells. The categories are assigned based on whether the travel district's average time and distance falls above or below the metropolitan average for the 194 travel districts of MCMZ. Finally, a one-way-ANOVA with post hoc analysis (Tukey's test) was conducted to identify any significant differences in average time and distance in the journey to work between the four categories of mobility situations.

Research results

Mobility situations by the numbers

Table 3.1 shows descriptive statistics for average time and distance in the journey to work, while Figures 3.1 and 3.2 show histograms with their distribution. The average travel time for MCMZ is 61.7 minutes, ranging from 42.9 minutes in the

Table 3.1 Average travel time and distance in the journey to work in the MCMZ, 2017

	Central tendency measures					*Percentiles*									*10/90 Ratio*
	Min	Max	Range	Mean	SD	10	20	30	40	50	60	70	80	90	
Time (minutes)	42.9	104.6	61.7	67.6	13.5	50.6	54.9	58.4	63.0	67.4	70.9	74.9	79.3	86.5	1.71
Distance (km)	4.7	30.7	26	11.7	4.5	6.9	7.6	8.7	10	10.7	11.8	13.5	15.6	18.3	2.65

Source: Author's calculations with data from the MCMZ 2017 Household Origin Destination Survey (INEGI)

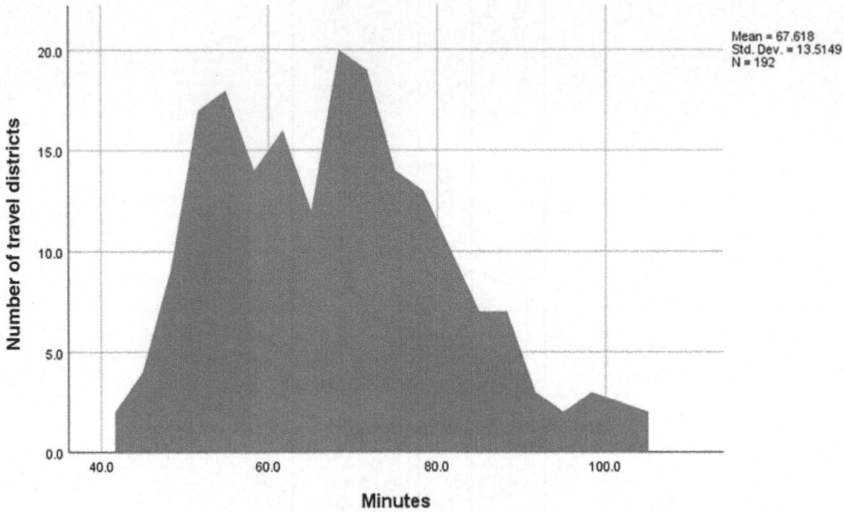

Source: Author's calculations based on the 2017 MVMZ Household Origin-Destination Survey, INEGI.

Figure 3.2 Average travel time histogram, 2017

travel district with the lowest time to 104.7 in the travel district with the highest time. The 10/90 ratio indicates that workers in the 90th percentile of the distribution need 1.71 times the time than workers in the 10th percentile. Average time is positively skewed, with most of the distribution needing between 50 and 75 minutes (Figure 3.2). The average travel distance for all MCMZ is 11.7 km, ranging from 4.7 km in the commuter zone with the lowest distance to 30.7 in that with the largest distance. The 10/90 ratio indicates that workers in the 90th percentile of the distribution travel 2.65 times the distance than workers in the 10th percentile. Average travel distance is positively skewed, with most of the distribution located between seven and 13 km (Figure 3.3).

Table 3.2 shows average time and distance in the journey to work by mobility situations. As the table shows, there is no significant difference in average commuting time between Short Commutes and Wormhole districts. Average time is 1.4 and 1.3 times longer in Long Commutes and Transit Hell districts, respectively, than in Short Commute districts. Travel time in Long Commutes takes 8.7 minutes more than in Transit Hells. As per average distance, there is no significant difference between Long Commutes and Wormholes. Average distance is 1.98 and 1.89 times longer in Long Commutes and Wormholes, respectively, than in Short Commutes. Average distance in Transit Hells is 2.2 km longer than in Short Commute districts.

The spatial distribution of mobility situations

Maps 3.1 and 3.2 show average travel time and distance in the journey to work, respectively. As per average time, the MCMZ territory is divided into five categories: low (42.9 to 53.8 minutes), medium-low (53.9 to 63.9 minutes),

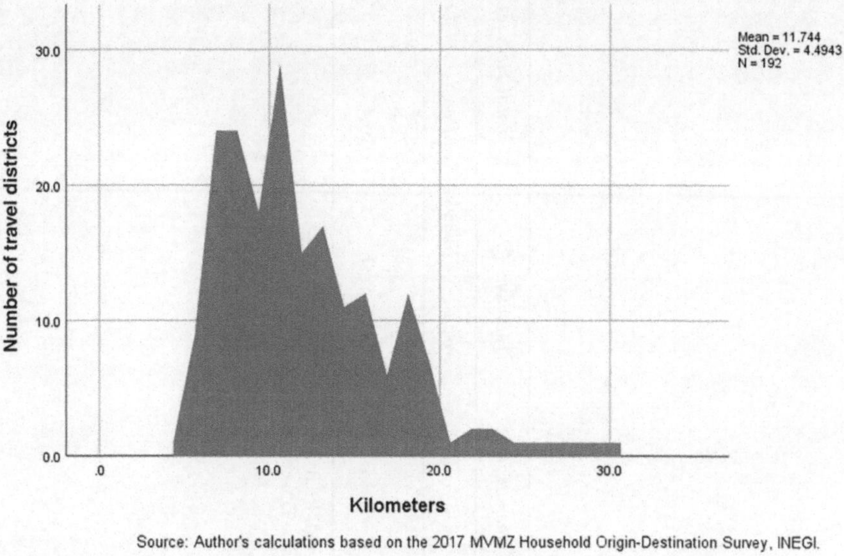

Figure 3.3 Average travel distance histogram, 2017

medium (64 to 74 minutes), medium-high (74.1 to 85.2 minutes), and high (85.3 to 104.7 minutes).[6] As shown in Map 3.1, the spatial distribution of the territories with the lowest and highest travel times in the journey to work shows a concentric pattern with a couple of notable exceptions. Concentric in the sense that the lowest travel times are at the center of the metropolitan region, and travel time increases as distance to the city center increases. This concentric spatial pattern holds throughout the region except for two territories. The first is along an area in the north-west of the State of Mexico, where a series of districts with low travel times stand out. A second territory that escapes the concentric pattern is in the urban periphery across the north, north-east, and south-east of the metropolitan region, also with low travel times.

In terms of average travel distance, Map 3.2 shows the five categories into which the territory has been classified: low (4.7 to 8.7 kilometers), medium-low (8.8 to 12 kilometers, medium (12.1 to 15.7 kilometers), medium-high (15.8 to 21 kilometers), and high (21.1 to 30.7 kilometers). As Map 3.2 shows, the spatial distribution of average distance also follows a concentric pattern. That is, there is a territory at the center of the metropolitan region with the lowest distance traveled. Then, the distance traveled increases with distance to the city center. The only exception to this concentric pattern is the western-most territory of the MCMZ, where commuters have some of the lowest average distances.

When the travel districts are classified into one of the four categories of mobility situations, Map 3.3 is obtained. As shown by the map, the spatial distribution of mobility situations follows a concentric pattern too. Most of the Short Commute zones are in the city center and toward the west and northwest of the urban region. This Short Commute zones are surrounded by Transit Hell zones. Most of the Transit Hells cluster in a corridor that borders Mexico City's central area. The Long

Table 3.2 Means, one way ANOVA and Tukey's test for differences by mobility situations

			Short Commutes (a)		*Long Commutes (b)*		*Wormholes (c)*		*Transit Hells (d)*	
	MCMZ mean	*ANOVA P*	*Mean*	*Tukey's*	*Mean*	*Tukey's*	*Mean*	*Tukey's*	*Mean*	*Tukey's*
Time (minutes)	67.6	<.001	56.5	c	81.5		58.8	a	72.8	
Distance (km)	11.7	<.001	8.2		16.3	c	15.5	b	10.4	

Source: Author's calculations with data from the MCMZ 2017 Household Origin Destination Survey (INEGI)
Note: The letters show where there is no significant difference between specific mobility. situations at a 95% confidence interval.

Commute zones are located beyond the Transit Hells. There are two salient clusters of Long Commute zones. The first is located at the north of the MCMZ. The second is located throughout Eastern-MCMZ. The rest of the Long Commute zones locate at the north and northwest of the MCMZ, and on the furthermost territories at the south of Mexico City. The Wormhole zones are located throughout three territories. The first is along the industrial corridor situated at the northwest of the urban region. The second is in the farthest northeastern territory. The third is situated in the utmost southeastern area of the MCMZ.

A closer look at the case study: Eastern-MCMZ

Map 3.4 shows the mobility situations in the travel districts within Eastern-MCMZ. Only two travel districts are classified as Short Commutes (177 and 178). These two districts are both the most proximate to the urban region's central area and the closest to available mass transport systems. They are also closer to the CETRAM Pantitlán, the main transit hub in the subregion with three subway lines that connect commuters with employment subcenters. The Short Commute districts are surrounded by a belt of Transit Hells (districts 176, 179, 180, and 181), while the rest of travel districts within Eastern-MCMZ are classified as Long Commutes. Map 3.4 also shows the scarce provision of mass public transport within Eastern-MCMZ, with only one subway line and one BRT line serving the subregion. Operating since 1991, only Line A of the subway serves the southern part of the subregion in the limits between Mexico City and the State of Mexico. As per BRT systems, the Line 3 of Mexibús System serves the northern part of the subregion since 2013.

Table 3.3 shows more information about the mobility situations in Eastern-MCMZ and its commuting patterns. While average commuting time for MCMZ is 67.7 minutes, the average time for Eastern-MCMZ is 83 minutes, with extreme cases such as travel districts 197 and 188 where average time is 104 and 99.9 minutes, respectively. While average commuting distance for MCMZ is 11.7 km, average distance for Eastern MCMZ is 15.1 km, with extreme cases such as travel districts 197 and 198 where average distance is 30.7 and 19.2 km, respectively. In terms of commuting patterns, Table 3.3 shows the percentage of trips with a destination within any of the urban region's employment subcenters[7] and the percentage of trips whose destination is within the same travel district of origin. While in MCMZ, 59.1 percent of the trips have as a destination an employment subcenter, in the case of Eastern-MCMZ, the figure goes down to 46.3 percent. This means that workers in Eastern-MCMZ have less access to the jobs located in employment subcenters than the average worker in the urban region.

Eastern-MCMZ also has fewer job opportunities because a smaller percentage of its workers remain within their same travel district of origin. While in MCMZ, 8.8 percent of workers find a job within their same travel district, in the case of Eastern-MCMZ, the figure goes down to 5.2 percent. Finally, Eastern-MCMZ is a subregion with important nuances in terms of commuting patterns and connectivity to jobs. For instance, some travel districts are relatively well

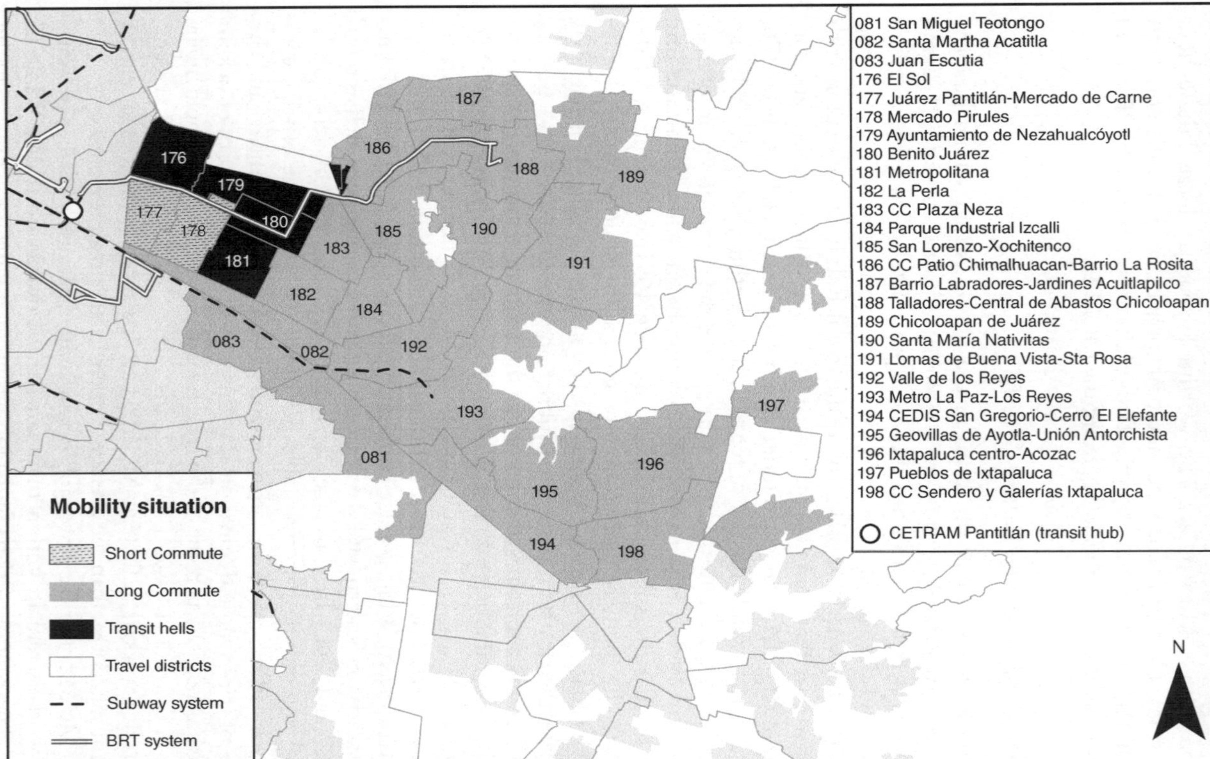

Source: Author's calculations with data from the MCMZ 2017 Origin-Destination Household Survey (EOD), INEGI.

Map 3.4 Travel districts and mobility situations in Eastern-MCMZ, 2017

Table 3.3 Mobility situations within Eastern-MCMZ, 2017

#	*Travel district*	*State*	*Mayoralty/ municipality*	*Average time (min)*	*Average distance (Km)*	*Mobility situation*	*Destination in employment subcenter (%)*	*Destination within origin travel district (%)*
	MCMZ	N/A	N/A	67.6	11.7	N/A	59.1	8.8
	Eastern-MCMZ	N/A	N/A	83.0	15.1	N/A	46.3	5.3
081	San Miguel Teotongo	Mexico City	Iztapalapa	81.6	14.5	Long Commute	50.8	5.5
082	Santa Martha Acatitla	Mexico City	Iztapalapa	72.8	13.1	Long Commute	53.5	4.4
083	Juan Escutia	Mexico City	Iztapalapa	71.4	11.9	Long Commute	53.9	3.8
176	El Sol	State of Mexico	Nezahualcoyotl	69.7	10.5	Transit Hells	51.6	6.1
177	Juárez Pantitlán-Mercado de Carne	State of Mexico	Nezahualcoyotl	66.6	10.5	Short Commute	59.6	1.6
178	Mercado Pirules	State of Mexico	Nezahualcoyotl	66.5	9.6	Short Commute	45.9	4.6
179	Ayuntamiento de Nezahualcóyotl	State of Mexico	Nezahualcoyotl	75.3	11.5	Transit Hells	48.1	7.2
180	Benito Juárez	State of Mexico	Nezahualcoyotl	72.2	11.1	Transit Hells	44.1	4.1
181	Metropolitana	State of Mexico	Nezahualcoyotl	75.1	11.3	Transit Hells	52.7	3.3
182	La Perla	State of Mexico	Nezahualcoyotl	78.6	12.7	Long Commute	49.1	4.3
183	CC Plaza Neza	State of Mexico	Nezahualcoyotl	76.5	11.8	Long Commute	46.8	5.6
184	Parque Industrial Izcalli	State of Mexico	Nezahualcoyotl	80.6	13.4	Long Commute	48.1	5.4
185	San Lorenzo-Xochitenco	State of Mexico	Chimalhuacán	92.4	14.6	Long Commute	44.4	1.7
186	CC Patio Chimalhuacán-Barrio La Rosita	State of Mexico	Chimalhuacán	83.6	14.3	Long Commute	46.6	2.6

(Continued)

Table 3.3 (Continued)

#	*Travel district*	*State*	*Mayoralty/ municipality*	*Average time (min)*	*Average distance (Km)*	*Mobility situation*	*Destination in employment subcenter (%)*	*Destination within origin travel district (%)*
187	Barrio Labradores-Jardines Acuitlapilco	State of Mexico	Chimalhuacán	89.1	16.2	Long Commute	42.7	3.1
188	Talladores-Central de Abastos Chicoloapan	State of Mexico	Chimalhuacán/ Chicoloapan	99.9	16.2	Long Commute	41.5	5.3
189	Chicoloapan de Juárez	State of Mexico	Chicoloapan/ Texcoco	91.0	18.0	Long Commute	45.6	9.2
190	Santa María Nativitas	State of Mexico	Chimalhuacán/ Chicoloapan	95.7	15.3	Long Commute	39.9	3.5
191	Lomas de Buena Vista-Sta Rosa	State of Mexico	Chimalhuacán/ Chicoloapan	98.7	18.6	Long Commute	35.1	4.4
192	Valle de los Reyes	State of Mexico	La Paz	86.5	15.1	Long Commute	43.6	4.6
193	Metro La Paz-Los Reyes	State of Mexico	La Paz	86.5	18.2	Long Commute	51.6	4.8
194	CEDIS San Gregorio-Cerro El Elefante	State of Mexico	Ixtapaluca	80.4	17.0	Long Commute	38.2	5.0
195	Geovillas de Ayotla-Unión Antorchista	State of Mexico	Ixtapaluca	88.1	19.0	Long Commute	39.5	8.4
196	Ixtapaluca centro-Acozac	State of Mexico	Ixtapaluca	89.8	17.1	Long Commute	45.2	11.8
197	Pueblos de Ixtapaluca	State of Mexico	Ixtapaluca	104.0	30.7	Long Commute	43.1	7.7
198	CC Sendero y Galerías Ixtapaluca	State of Mexico	Ixtapaluca	86.5	19.2	Long Commute	42.6	10.4

Source: Author's calculations with data from the MCMZ 2017 Household Origin Destination Survey (INEGI) connected to jobs in employment subcenters—for example, 082, 083, and 177, while others are poorly connected—for example, 191 and 194. Some travel districts, especially those further into the peripheral area, are able to retain a larger share of their workforce—for example, 196 and 198, while other travel districts retain a very small share of its workers—for example, 177 and 185.

Conclusions

This chapter presented a study of time and distance in the journey to work to identify diverging mobility situations in MCMZ in general, and in Eastern-MCMZ in particular. The study allowed to identify that mobility situations in MCMZ show a concentric pattern. Tracts with the best mobility situation, a Short Commute, are mainly located at the center, west, and northwest of the urban region. A belt of Transit Hells surrounds and encircles the Short Commute areas. Peripheral areas are composed of a patchwork of Long Commutes and Wormhole districts. Eastern-MCMZ has some of the highest average times and distances in the journey to work and is composed mainly of Long Commute travel districts.

This chapter serves as the backdrop within which the following empirical studies presented in Chapters 4, 5, and 6 should be interpreted. The purpose of the following three chapters is to explore why and how Eastern-MCMZ has been configured as a geography of low accessibility to jobs with some of the worst mobility situations across the urban region. By investigating shifts in the spatial location of the demand for labor, Chapter 4 explores the contribution of economic development policies to the proximity between jobs and workers. By researching the housing pathways available for workers in the case study, Chapter 5 investigates the contributions of housing policy in increasing the physical distance between jobs and workers in the case study. Finally, Chapter 6 takes a closer look the political economy of public transport in Eastern-MCMZ.

Notes

1 The geographical breakdown of the travel districts can be seen in: http://giitral.iingen.unam.mx/Estudios/EstudioOD-ZMVM-2017.html

2 There are new and emerging trends in the journey to work that are out of the scope of the empirical investigation in this book but should be kept in mind for future research efforts. For example, the journey to work is often combined with other activities. This is specially the case of women who use their journey to work to perform other activities related with the care of the household. This opens the possibility for studies of the journey to work through a feminist urbanism perspective. Another trend that should be kept in mind is the implications of the structural transformation of urban-based economic activities from formal jobs to self-employment. This means that, increasingly, the journey to work is less bound to a single and stable destination and is becoming more fluid. To these trends, we can add the journey to work derived from informal economic activities in the city, which also have a less fixed and stable destination and are fluid too.

3 Segmenting a survey to analyze cases within specific categories comes with the risk of reducing the representativeness of the sample, thus making the sampling error greater. Nevertheless, to avoid making groups that are too small within the process of

segmentation, statisticians recommend applying size filters in which segmentation is stopped when a group falls below a predetermined threshold in the number of cases. As a general rule, the specialists in sampling methods recommend a threshold of 50 cases per group to secure representativeness (Diáz de Rada, 2009; Escobar, 1998). There was only one travel district that, after the segmentation, ended up with 36 cases and therefore its data cannot be considered representative of the travel district. I am referring to travel district 056 "Las Lomas," which after segmentation was removed from the study.

4 Following Niedzielski and Boschmann (2014), estimating the median travel time, as opposed to the mean, helps to best identify the central tendency of travel time within each district-to-district combination with observed flow of trips. Subsequent steps of the methodology aggregate data based on averages of median travel time.

5 Weighting the average by the number of trips in each combination of district-to-district pair allows preventing any bias due to outliers in the median travel time. This is so because weighting the mean by the number of trips assigns more weight to the combinations of origins and destinations with more trips and less weight to the combinations with fewer trips.

6 The categories in Maps 3.1 and 3.2 were created based on the natural breaks of the data's distribution with help of geographical information systems (GIS).

7 The identification of employment subcenters is carefully explained in Chapter 4.

References

Blumenberg, E., Pierce, G., & Smart, M. (2015). Transportation access, residential location, and economic opportunity: Evidence from two housing voucher experiments. *Cityscape: A Journal of Policy Development and Research, 17*(2), 89–111.

Bocarejo, J. P., & Oviedo, D. R. (2012). Transport accessibility and social inequities: A tool for identification of mobility needs and evaluation of transport investments. *Journal of Transport Geography, 24*, 142–154.

Clark, B., Chatterjee, K., Martin, A., & Davis, A. (2020). How commuting affects subjective wellbeing. *Transportation, 47*(6), 2777–2805.

Diáz de Rada, V. (2009). *Análisis de datos de encuestas: Desarrollo de una investigación completa utilizando SPSS*. Barcelona: Editorial UOC.

Escobar, M. (1998). *Las aplicaciones del análisis de segmentación: El procedimiento CHAD Instituto Juan March de Estudios e Investigaciones*. Universidad Carlos III.

Geurs, K. T., & van Wee, B. (2004). Accessibility evaluation of land-use and transport strategies: Review and research directions. *Journal of Transport Geography, 12*(2), 127–140.

Grengs, J. (2012). Equity and the social distribution of job accessibility in Detroit. *Environment and Planning B: Planning and Design, 39*, 785–800.

Handy, S. L., & Niemeier, D. A. (1997). Measuring accessibility: An exploration of issues and alternatives. *Environment and Planning A, 29*, 1175–1194.

Kahneman, D., Krueger, A. B., Schkade, D. A., Schwarz, N., & Stone, A. A. (2004). A survey method for characterizing daily life experience: The day reconstruction method. *Science, 306*(5702), 1776–1780.

Niedzielski, M. A., & Boschmann, E. E. (2014). Travel time and distance as relative accessibility in the journey to work. *Annals of the Association of American Geographers, 104*, 1156–1182.

Ong, P. M., & Miller, D. (2005). Spatial and transportation mismatch in Los Angeles. *Journal of Planning Education and Research, 25*(1), 43–56.

Páez, A., Scott, D. M., & Morency, C. (2012). Measuring accessibility: Positive and normative implementations of various accessibility indicators. *Journal of Transport Geography, 25*, 141–153.

Shen, Q. (1998). Location characteristics of inner-city neighborhoods and employment accessibility of low-wage workers. *Environment and Planning B: Planning and Design, 25*(3), 345–365.

van Wee, B., & Geurs, K. T. (2011). Discussing equity and social exclusion in accessibility evaluations. *European Journal of Transport and Infrastructure Research, 11*(4), 350–367.

4 Shifts in the spatial location of the demand for labor, 1999–2019

It is intuitive to think that the mobility experience of workers in urban regions is mainly determined by the availability of transport systems. This is partially true, but there is more to it. To really understand what shapes the mobility experience of workers, in addition to transport systems, one must also consider the spatial distribution and the sorting of commuting origins and destinations. When commuting, the origins of trips tend to be the residential location of workers. The destinations have to do with the places that commuters are trying to reach. I will deal with the origins of the trips—that is, the residential location of workers—in Chapter 5. For now, this chapter will deal with the destinations of trips: the places where jobs are located and where commuters are trying to arrive at. The spatial distribution of destinations in urban regions is influenced, at least, by the kinds of economic activities supported by cities, the legacies of past infrastructures and land-use policies, the aggregation of myriads of individual location decisions by firms, and the strategic actions of urban actors with an interest in influencing the location of jobs. The interplay between all these factors operates to concentrate jobs in specific places that commuters must then reach.

The concentration of jobs across space provides urban regions with an urban structure. Scholars distinguish between regions structured around a sole concentration of jobs—the monocentric urban structure—or around several employment subcenters—the polycentric city. Furthermore, scholars are interested in assessing if an urban region is trending toward a monocentric urban structure or toward a polycentric one. The urban structure has implications for the mobility experience of workers. In monocentric cities, commuters from across the urban region try to reach the single employment subcenter. This, in turn, puts pressure over existing transit infrastructures. In a polycentric urban structure, the several employment subcenters attract commuters from across the urban region. This, in turn, can produce friction across existing transport systems due to the dispersion between origins and destinations.

This chapter argues that shifts in the spatial location of the demand for labor partially determines the mobility experience of workers. The chapter investigates shifts in the spatial location of the demand for labor in MCMZ between 1999 and 2019. By replicating a widely used methodology for the study of

DOI: 10.4324/9781003261698-4

economic geographies, the chapter presents an analysis of employment magnitude and density for the identification of employment subcenters. Economic specialization indexes are calculated to assess the main economic activity and the kind of jobs present in each employment subcenter. Additionally, a primacy index is calculated to assess whether the MCMZ is trending toward a monocentric or a polycentric urban form. Finally, semi-structured interviews with 34 key informants allow to identify some of the urban policies driving the shifts in the spatial location of the demand for labor.

The main finding of the chapter is that, despite the MCMZ achieving to generate more employment subcenters, from 22 in 1999 to 29 in 2019, and the primacy index indicating that MCMZ is trending toward a polycentric urban form, from 3.44 in 1999 to 2.26 in 2019, the formal jobs available in MCMZ are concentrating in space. In 1999, 52.8 percent of the jobs available in the metropolitan region were concentrated in 9.3 percent of its territory. By 2019, 58.5 percent of the jobs were concentrated in 8.4 percent of the territory. Furthermore, most of the new employment subcenters and those agglomerations moving up in the urban hierarchy are in the center, west, and northwest of the metropolitan region. The shift in the geographies of jobs keeps operating to the disadvantage of the population of Eastern-MCMZ.

The chapter identified four distinct factors that have contributed to a concentration of jobs toward the central, west, and northwest areas of the MCMZ, and away from Eastern-MCMZ. First, the geographies of jobs sparked by the Mexican economic miracle that occurred between the 1940s and the 1960s continue to have an influence over current economic geographies. Second, the varying land-use regulations across urban space attract productive investment toward the central, west, and northwest of the MCMZ, while failing to attract new investment into Eastern-MCMZ. Third, there seems to be a symbolic dimension among entrepreneurs that stigmatizes the Eastern-MCMZ as an undesirable location for large-scale investment. And fourth, specific state-led megaprojects have proved to be at work behind the reinforcement of employment subcenters away from Eastern-MCMZ.

Analytical strategy and research methods

The articles by Muñiz et al. (2003), García and Muñiz (2005), Garrocho and Campos (2007), and Aguilar and Hernández (2012) provide a thorough overview of the available methodologies for the identification of employment subcenters. Such methodologies allow an empirical assessment of urban structure. In summary, there are six different methodologies: a priori knowledge of the area of study (Baerwald, 1982; Cervero, 1989; Erickson, 1986; Green, 1980), analysis of commuting flows (Bourne, 1989; Clark & Kuijpers-Linde, 1994; Gordon & Richardson, 1996), employment magnitude and density thresholds (Cervero & Wu, 1997; Giuliano & Small, 1991; McMillen & McDonald, 1997), employment density peaks (Craig & Ng, 2001; Gordon et al., 1986; McDonald, 1987; McDonald & McMillen, 1990), positive residuals in an econometric estimation (McDonald & Prather, 1994; McMillen, 2001, 2003; McMillen & Smith, 2003), and exploring data with spatial econometrics techniques (Baumont et al., 2004; Guillain et al., 2004; Montejano et al., 2016).

The selection of any of these methods depends on research goals, data availability, the spatial scale of the analysis, and the local context of the city under study (Aguilar & Hernández, 2012). Techniques based on econometric estimations are recommended when the goal is to compare urban form among a sample of cities. The use of methodologies based on employment magnitude and density thresholds is recommended when the purpose is to study the evolution of urban form in one city across several points in time (Aguilar & Hernández, 2012: p. 216).

The goal of this study is to assess shifts in the special location of the demand for labor in MCMZ urban form between 1999 and 2019. To do so, this study resorts to the *employment magnitude and density threshold* method as originally proposed by Giuliano and Small (1991) and applied to Mexican cities by Garrocho and Campos (2007), Aguilar and Hernández (2012), and López-García and Gómez-Álvarez (2022). The data for this study were provided by the Microdata Lab of the National Institute of Statistics, Geography and Informatics (INEGI, by its acronym in Spanish) under data request LM-1726. The Microdata Lab provided data from the 1999 and 2019 Economic Census on the number of workers employed by census tract for the MCMZ by type of economic sector (manufacturing, commerce, and services) and by type of job (operative, managerial, outsourced, and contract).

The employment magnitude and density threshold method consists of two steps. The first step identifies the census tracts that exceed the following thresholds:

1 An employment magnitude above the mean of the city under study, plus one standard deviation.
2 An employment density above the mean of the city under study.

These criteria guarantee that the identified census tracts will show employment magnitude and density values that are atypically high with respect to the spatial distribution of employment (Aguilar & Hernández, 2012; Garrocho & Campos, 2007). Following Aguilar and Hernández (2012), the formula to identify the census tracts that exceed both thresholds is the following:

$$\text{D}i,\ s > \text{D}c,\ st$$
$$\text{M}i,\ s > (\text{E}c,\ s,\ t) + (\text{SD E}c,\ s,\ t)$$

where:

D = Employment density (Jobs/Hectare)
i = Census tract

s = Sectoral aggregation
c = City under study
t = year of the analysis
M = Employment magnitude (number of jobs)
E = Average employment magnitude per census tract
SD = Standard Deviation

The thresholds used in this study, as well as other thresholds used in similar studies for Mexican cities, such as the study of Garrocho and Campos (2007) for Toluca, Aguilar and Hernández (2012) for Mexico City, and López-García and Gómez-Álvarez (2022) for Guadalajara, can be seen in Table 4.1. Following the steps of Aguilar and Hernández (2012), three categories of census tracts were built. The census tracts concentrating employment between one and two standard deviations from the mean are classified as *moderate* concentration.

Table 4.1 Thresholds for the identification of census tracts that concentrate employment in Mexican cities

Year	*Number of census tracts*	*Employment magnitude*			*Employment density*
		Average	*Standard deviation*	*Threshold (number of jobs)*	*Threshold (jobs/ha)*
Mexico City Metropolitan Zone (MCMZ) Thresholds for this study					
1999	4,391	708.5	1,410.4	2,118.9	23.7
2019	6,059	921.5	2,109.7	3,031.2	28.0
Mexico City Metropolitan Zone (MCMZ), Aguilar & Hernández, 2012					
1989	3,455	545.1	1,512.6	2,057.7	15.7
1994	4,309	584.5	1,334.4	1,918.9	29.6
1999	4,505	640.0	1,441.0	2,081.0	20.5
2004	5,433	630.0	1,728.0	2,358.0	19.4
Toluca Metropolitan Area (AMT), Garrocho & Campos, 2007					
1994	n/d	n/d	n/d	1,524	6.3
1999	n/d	n/d	n/d	1,587	8.6
2004	n/d	n/d	n/d	1,339	7.6
Guadalajara Metropolitan Area (AMG), López-García & Gómez-Álvarez, 2022.					
1999	1,140	668.1	1,214.7	1,883	18.1
2019	2,037	833.9	1,549.9	2,384	21.7

Source: The thresholds for this study were calculated by the authors with data from the 1999 and 2019 Economic Census provided by the National Institute of Statistics, Geography and Informatics (INEGI). The rest of the thresholds were taken from Garrocho and Campos (2007), Aguilar and Hernández (2012), and López-García and Gómez-Álvarez (2022).

Those concentrating employment between two and three standard deviations from the mean are classified as *high* concentration. Finally, the census tracts concentrating employment more than three standard deviations from the mean are classified as *very high* concentration.

The second step of the methodology analyzes the spatial structure of the census tracts that concentrate employment, aiming to identify the areas that can be considered an employment subcenter. Giuliano and Small (1991: p. 166) define an employment subcenter as a continuous set of zones, each with employment magnitude and density above some cutoff threshold and for which all the immediately adjacent zones have employment magnitude and density below the threshold. To be classified as adjacent, the zones must have at least 0.25 miles of a common boundary (400 meters). Through this criterion, all the census tracts that concentrate employment and are adjacent to each other are classified as part of an employment subcenter, unless they are isolated and do not form part of any continuous set of census tracts. Once the employment subcenters were identified, I analyzed their size to rank them according to their hierarchy within the urban structure. Local specialization indexes were calculated to assess the main economic sector and the type of jobs prevalent in each employment subcenter.[1] Additionally, a primacy index was calculated to assess whether the MCMZ is trending toward a monocentric or a polycentric urban form.[2]

It is worth mentioning the limitations of this method to assess urban form of Mexican cities. The main weakness is that the method fails to take into account informal economic activity, which is one of the most important characteristics of Latin American cities (Roy & AlSayyad, 2003; Ward, 2019). The lack of systematic and reliable data on informal economic activity is the main obstacle to incorporating these kinds of jobs into the analysis of employment subcenters. Informal economic activity is one of the main sources of employment in Latin American cities and one that ought to be included in studies of urban structure.

Research results

Map 4.1 shows the census tracts that surpass the employment magnitude and density thresholds in 1999, while Map 4.2 shows the results for 2019. As can be seen in Table 4.2, in 1999, the 75 mayoralties and municipalities of the MCMZ comprised a total of 4,391 census tracts that in 168,250.6 hectares provided 3,402,611 jobs. That year, only 332 census tracts exceeded the methodology's thresholds, which in 15,720.6 hectares concentrated 1,796,827 jobs. Taken together, these tracts concentrated 52.8 percent of the jobs available in the MCMZ in 1999 in 9.3 percent of its territory. As Map 4.2 shows, most of the census tracts concentrating employment in 1999 were in the center and northwest of the metropolitan region.

As per 2019, Table 4.2 shows that the MCMZ comprised 6,059 tracts which in a total of 229,107.8 hectares provided 5,036,679 jobs. That year, the number

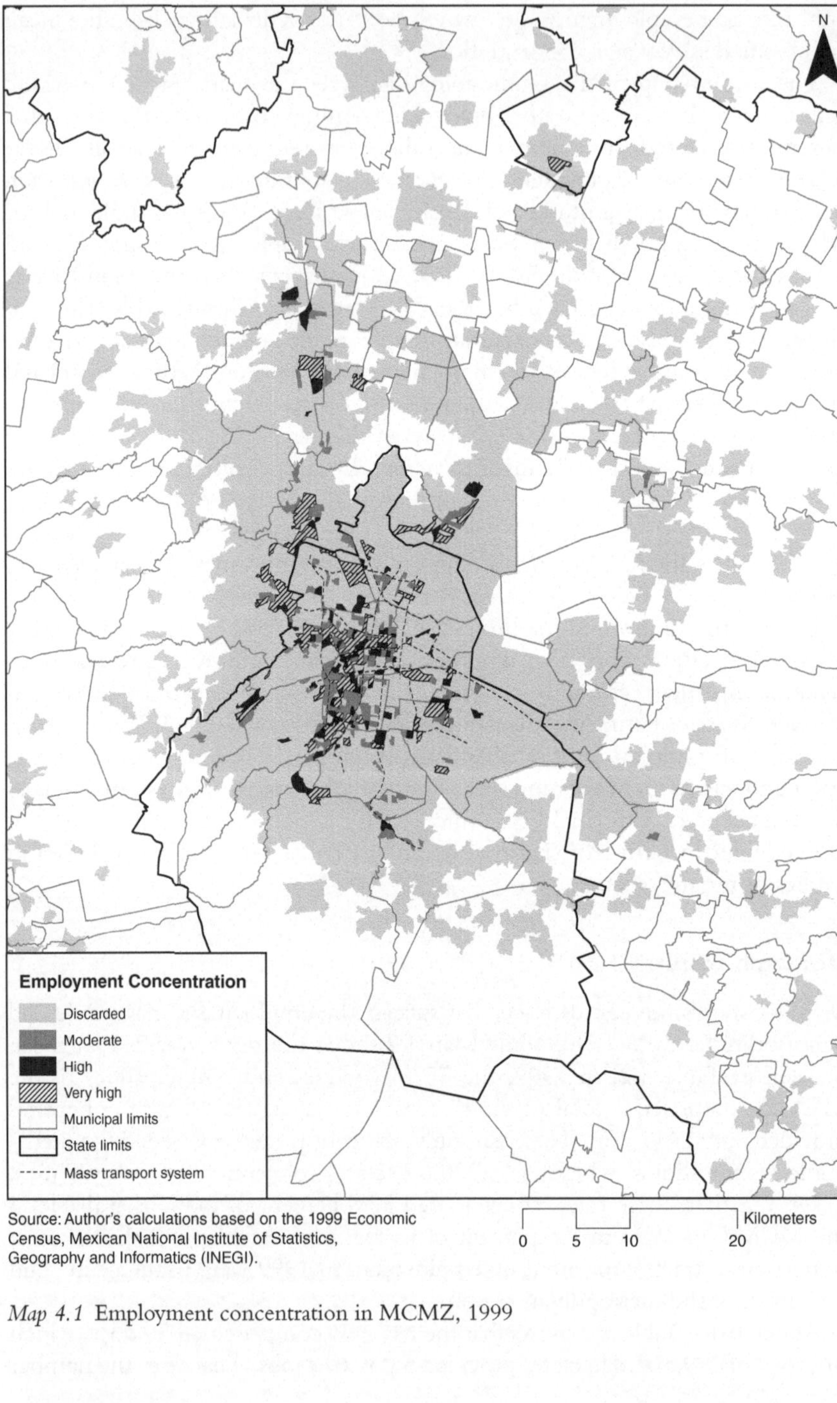

Source: Author's calculations based on the 1999 Economic Census, Mexican National Institute of Statistics, Geography and Informatics (INEGI).

Map 4.1 Employment concentration in MCMZ, 1999

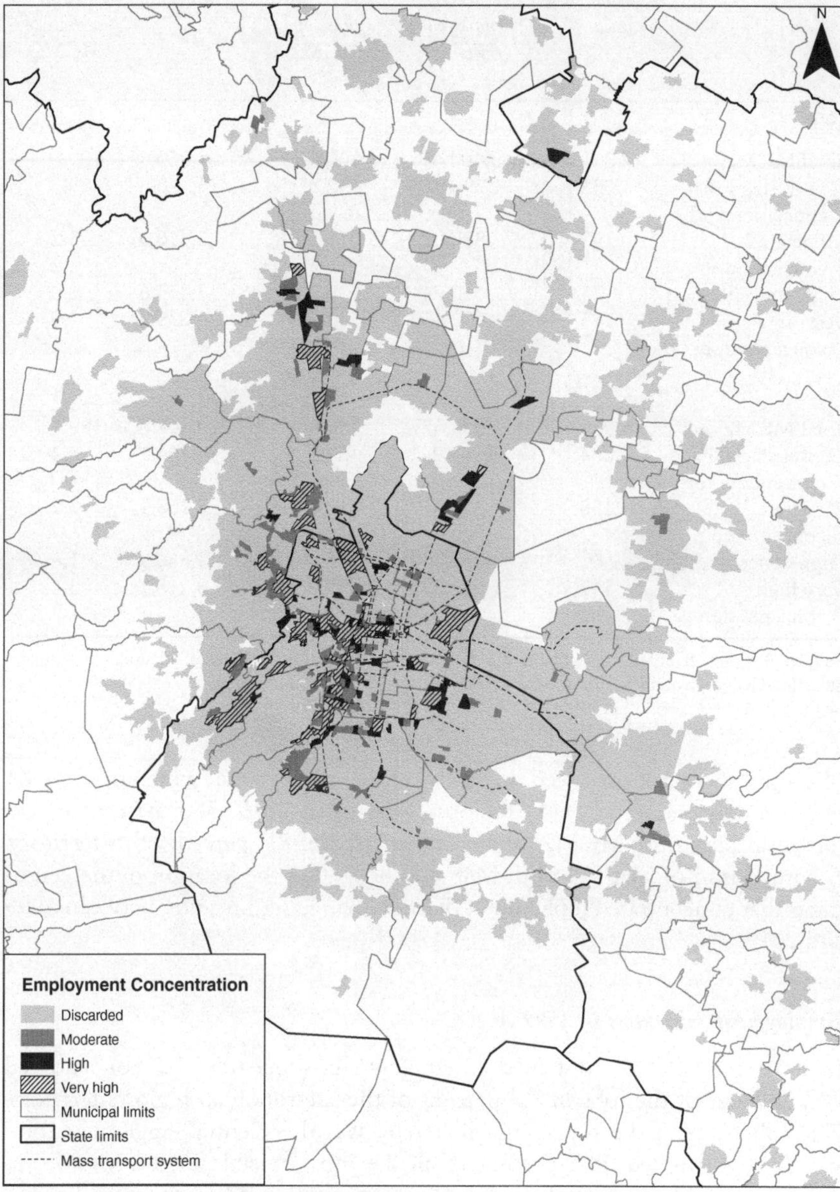

Source: Author's calculations based on the 2019 Economic Census, Mexican National Institute of Statistics, Geography and Informatics (INEGI).

Map 4.2 Employment concentration in MCMZ, 2019

Table 4.2 Census tracts that concentrate employment in the MCMZ, 1999 and 2019[3]

	# of census tracts	*Workers employed (WE)*	*WE as a share of MCMZ (%)*	*Area (Ha)*	*Area as a share of MCMZ (%)*
1999					
Total MCMZ	4,391	3,402,611	100.0	168,250.6	100
Census tracts that concentrate jobs	332	1,796,827	52.8	15,720.6	9.3
Moderate concentration	142	386,023	11.3	5,410.0	3.2
High concentration	75	310,344	9.1	3,474.6	2.0
Very high concentration	115	1,100,460	32.3	6,835.9	4.0
2019					
Total MCMZ	6,059	5,036,679	100.0	229,107.8	100
Census tracts that concentrate jobs	334	2,944,211	58.5	19,164.1	8.4
Moderate concentration	158	623,359	12.4	7,365.1	3.2
High concentration	59	358,254	5.9	3,580.9	1.6
Very high concentration	117	1,962,597	39.0	8,218.1	3.6

Source: Author's elaboration based on the 1999 and 2019 Economic Census, National Institute of Statistics, Geography and Informatics (INEGI)

of census tracts that surpassed the study's threshold was 334, which in 19,164.1 hectares concentrated 2,944,211 jobs. That is, in 2019, 58.5 percent of the jobs available in the MCMZ were concentrated in 8.4 percent of its territory. A comparison of Map 4.1 with Map 4.2 shows that the location of the census tracts that concentrate employment did not change significantly between 1999 and 2019.

Employment subcenters in 1999

In 1999, the MCMZ contained 22 employment subcenters that concentrated 44.7 percent of the jobs in 7.3 percent of the metropolitan region's territory. The subcenter at the top of the hierarchy was the Central Agglomeration,[4] which concentrated 28.7 percent of all the jobs available in the MCMZ in 3.2 percent of the metropolitan region's territory. This subcenter specialized in the service sector and provided mainly outsourced jobs. In 1999, the Central Agglomeration was, by far, the most important economic agglomeration in MCMZ.

The second employment subcenter in the hierarchy of 1999 was Naucalpan, which concentrated 3.1 percent of the MCMZ jobs, had a manufacturing economic specialization, and provided mainly managerial jobs. The third employment subcenter in the hierarchy was Tlalnepantla, which concentrated 2.5 percent of the city's jobs, had an economic specialization in the manufacturing sector, and offered mainly operative jobs. The fourth employment subcenter in the hierarchy was Mercado de Abastos (the MCMZ main fresh produce wholesale market), which concentrated 1.5 percent of the available jobs in the city, had an economic specialization in commerce, and provided operative jobs. The fifth employment subcenter in the hierarchy was Iztacalco 1, which concentrated 1.3 percent of the city's jobs, had a manufacturing economic specialization, and provided operative jobs. Tables 4.3 and 4.4 offer a summary of the rest of employment subcenters in 1999.

Table 4.3 Employment subcenters in MCMZ, 1999

Subcenter	*Number of census tracts*	*Workers employed (WE)*	*WE as a share of MCMZ (%)*	*Area (Ha)*	*Area as a share of MCMZ (%)*	*Density (WE/Ha)*
1. Central Agglomeration	176	975,807	28.7	5,364.6	3.19	181.9
2. Naucalpan	13	104,185	3.1	850.4	0.51	122.5
3. Tlalnepantla	13	84,707	2.5	1,045.9	0.62	81.0
4. Mercado de Abastos	7	49,658	1.5	562.8	0.33	88.2
5. Iztacalco 1	5	45,470	1.3	244.5	0.15	186.0
6. Azcapotzalco 1	2	44,720	1.3	395.2	0.23	113.2
7. Ecatepec	8	38,146	1.1	595.8	0.35	64.0
8. Cuautitlán 1	4	28,807	0.8	518.9	0.31	55.5
9. Perisur	4	24,241	0.7	434.3	0.26	55.8
10. Acapotzalco/ Cuauhtémoc	4	18,874	0.6	157.3	0.09	120.0
11. Santa Fe	3	14,472	0.4	393.4	0.23	36.8
12. Azcapotzalco 2	3	13,338	0.4	155.3	0.09	85.9
13. Coyoacán	3	13,042	0.4	244.8	0.15	53.3
14. Iztacalco 2	2	9,584	0.3	112.1	0.07	85.5
15. Gustavo A. Madero 1	2	8,734	0.3	102.8	0.06	85.0
16. Iztapalapa 2	2	7,755	0.2	87.3	0.05	88.8
17. Xochimilco	2	7,706	0.2	192.4	0.11	40.1
18. Tepotzotlán	2	7,170	0.2	249.7	0.15	28.7
19. Cuautitlán 2	2	7,066	0.2	249.3	0.15	28.3
20. Álvaro Obregón	2	6,451	0.2	53.0	0.03	121.7
21. Gustavo A. Madero 2	2	5,443	0.2	148.3	0.09	36.7
22. Tlalpan	2	5,293	0.2	75.4	0.04	70.2
Total subcenters	263	1,520,669	44.7	12,233.4	7.3	–
Total MCMZ	4,391	3,402,611	100	168,250.6	100	20.2

Source: Author's calculations based on the 1999 Economic Census, National Institute of Statistics, Geography and Informatics (INEGI)

Table 4.4 Employment subcenters' specialization indexes for economic sector and type of job, MCMZ, 1999

Subcenter	*Economic sector*			*Type of jobs*		
	Manu-facturing	*Commerce*	*Services*	*Operative*	*Manage-rial*	*Outsourced*
1. Central Agglomeration	0.56	0.96	1.23	0.90	0.92	1.19
2. Naucalpan	2.29	0.82	0.35	1.17	1.23	0.67
3. Tlalnepantla	1.75	1.13	0.63	1.22	1.04	0.79
4. Mercado de Abastos	0.52	2.68	0.81	0.92	1.33	0.54
5. Iztacalco 1	2.54	0.43	0.32	1.35	0.85	0.48
6. Azcapotzalco 1	1.77	0.81	0.77	1.10	1.35	0.60
7. Ecatepec	2.51	0.69	0.22	1.25	1.03	0.44
8. Cuautitlán 1	2.48	0.72	0.23	1.32	0.99	0.62
9. Perisur	0.24	1.28	1.25	1.17	1.04	0.69
10. Acapotzalco/ Cuauhtémoc	2.23	1.01	0.30	1.23	1.20	0.18
11. Santa Fe	0.39	1.86	1.39	1.01	1.73	2.97
12. Azcapotzalco 2	1.81	0.98	0.65	1.01	1.48	0.22
13. Coyoacán	0.85	0.69	1.58	1.06	1.44	0.51
14. Iztacalco 2	1.94	1.10	0.49	1.32	0.85	0.29
15. Gustavo A. Madero 1	2.27	1.08	0.23	1.30	0.97	0.77
16. Iztapalapa 2	2.16	0.89	0.42	1.17	1.28	1.33
17. Xochimilco	2.10	0.26	0.77	1.01	1.55	0.28
18. Tepotzotlán	2.02	1.39	0.28	1.33	0.80	0.97
19. Cuautitlán 2	2.22	0.43	0.58	1.32	0.91	0.21
20. Álvaro Obregón	1.07	0.51	1.48	0.99	1.20	0.33
21. Gustavo A. Madero 2	0.51	1.17	1.62	1.41	0.63	0.66
22. Tlalpan	0.21	3.17	0.90	1.46	0.28	0.69

Source: Author's calculations based on the 1999 Economic Census, National Institute of Statistics, Geography and Informatics (INEGI)

Map 4.3 shows the location of the employment subcenters identified in 1999. Except for Ecatepec, Iztacalco 1 and 2, Iztapalapa 1 and 2, Tlalpan, and Xochimilco, the rest of the employment subcenters are in the center and northwest of the metropolitan region.

Employment subcenters in 2019

Table 4.5 shows that in 2019, the MCMZ contained 29 employment subcenters that in 15,326 hectares concentrated 2,615,694 jobs. These subcenters concentrated 51.9 percent of all the jobs available in 2019 into 6.69 percent of the metropolitan region's territory. The Central Agglomeration continued

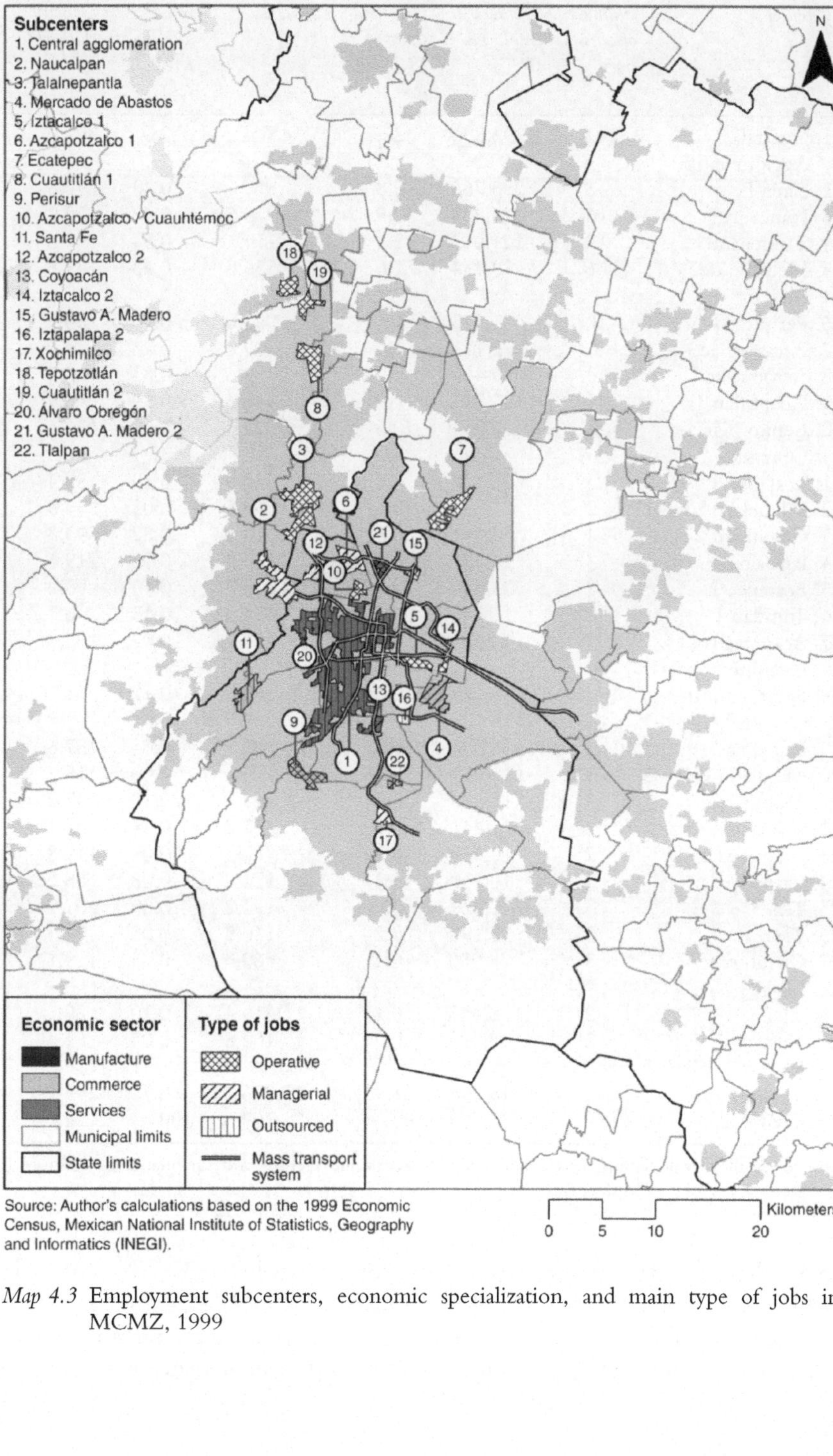

Map 4.3 Employment subcenters, economic specialization, and main type of jobs in MCMZ, 1999

Table 4.5 Employment subcenters in MCMZ, 2019

Subcenter	*Number of census tracts*	*Workers employed (WE)*	*WE as a share of MCMZ (%)*	*Area (Ha)*	*Area as a share of MCMZ (%)*	*Density (WE/Ha)*
1. Central Agglomeration	146	1,393,806	27.7	4,631	2.0	301.0
2. Santa Fe	8	293,766	5.8	987	0.43	297.6
3. Naucalpan	16	126,464	2.5	973.5	0.42	129.9
4. Tlalnepantla	17	121,013	2.4	1,239.3	0.54	97.6
5. Mercado de Abastos	6	80,334	1.6	536.3	0.23	149.8
6. Perisur	10	74,375	1.5	923.8	0.40	80.5
7. Azcapotzalco 1	4	72,111	1.4	599.6	0.26	120.3
8. Aeropuerto	2	49,460	1.0	754.6	0.33	65.5
9. Cuautitlán 1	4	43,234	0.9	446	0.19	96.9
10. Benito Juárez/ Obregón	5	28,253	0.6	224	0.10	126.1
11. Ecatepec 1	5	26,178	0.5	440.9	0.19	59.4
12. Miguel Hidalgo 1	2	24,592	0.5	69.5	0.03	353.8
13. Cuautitlán 2	4	22,141	0.4	510.9	0.22	43.3
14. Iztacalco	3	21,489	0.4	180.4	0.08	119.1
15. Ecatepec 2	2	21,080	0.4	219.7	0.10	95.9
16. Tultitlán 1	2	16,545	0.3	354.2	0.15	46.7
17. Acapotzalco/ Cuauhtémoc	4	16,503	0.3	157.2	0.07	105.0
18. Huixquilucan/ Cuajimalpa	2	16,198	0.3	265.6	0.12	61.0
19. Ecatepec 3	2	15,386	0.3	97.6	0.04	157.6
20. Miguel Hidalgo 2	3	15,058	0.3	129	0.06	116.7
21. Tepotzotlán	3	14,504	0.3	307	0.13	47.2
22. Tultitlán 2	2	11,441	0.2	317.2	0.14	36.1
23. Iztapalapa 2	2	10,459	0.2	87.3	0.04	119.8
24. Iztapalapa 3	2	10,250	0.2	176	0.08	58.2
25. Texcoco	3	10,229	0.2	197.2	0.09	51.9
26. Tlalpan	3	10,198	0.2	110.5	0.05	92.3
27. Cuauhtémoc/ Juárez	2	8,950	0.2	69.3	0.03	129.1
28. Chalco	2	8,443	0.2	219.4	0.10	38.5
29. Gustavo A. Madero	2	8,393	0.2	102.8	0.04	81.6
Total subcenters	268	2,615,694	51.9	15,326	6.7	–
Total MCMZ	6,059	5,036,679	100	229,107.8	100	22.0

Source: Author's calculations based on the 2019 Economic Census and the National Institute of Statistics, Geography and Informatics (INEGI)

to be the employment subcenter at the top of the hierarchy, concentrating 1,393,806 jobs, or 27.7 percent of the available jobs in 2 percent of the urban region's territory. A salient characteristic of the Central Agglomeration is that it became smaller in area but with a denser employment concentration. The employment density of the Central Agglomeration increased from 181.9 jobs per hectare in 1999 to 301 in 2019. This subcenter continued to have an economic specialization in the services sector, and the main type of jobs available were contract jobs.

The second subcenter in the hierarchy of 2019, Santa Fe, is a striking surprise of the study. Created in the 1990s as the paragon of Mexico City's globalization, the number of jobs in Santa Fe grew from 14,472 jobs in 1999, to 293,766 in 2019. This allowed Santa Fe to move from the eleventh employment subcenter in the hierarchy of 1999 to the second in the hierarchy of 2019. With a specialization in the service sector, most of the jobs offered in Santa Fe are managerial. The next employment subcenters in the hierarchy of 2019 were Naucalpan, Tlalnepantla, and Mercado de Abastos, respectively. Naucalpan and Tlalnepantla continued to be the two most important subcenters in the manufacturing economic sector and remain to specialize in operative and outsourced jobs, respectively. Mercado de Abastos specializes in commerce but shows no specialization in the kind of jobs provided by this subcenter. The sixth employment subcenter in the hierarchy of 2019 is another outstanding finding of the study: Perisur. In 1999, Perisur was the ninth employment subcenter of the hierarchy. By 2019, Perisur moved to the sixth place. With an economic specialization in the service sector, the jobs available in Perisur are mainly contract jobs.

Map 4.4 shows the spatial location of the employment subcenters identified in 2019. There are several features to highlight about the urban structure of MCMZ in 2019 in comparison to 1999. First, the Central Agglomeration is becoming longer and slimmer. Second, Santa Fe and Perisur are increasing their size and moving up in the urban hierarchy. Third, most of the new employment subcenters are in the State of Mexico. The industrial corridor located at the northwest of the metropolitan region gained two more employment subcenters. The eastern-most part of the MCMZ also gained two employment subcenters, Texcoco and Chalco. This can be interpreted as good news for eastern MCMZ, a zone that has traditionally lagged in terms of socioeconomic development. However, with 10,229 and 8,443 jobs, respectively, Texcoco and Chalco occupy the twenty-fifth and twenty-eighth places in the hierarchy.

Trending toward polycentrism with increased job concentration

Table 4.7 provides primacy indexes in MCMZ for 2, 3, 4, and 5 employment subcenters. In all cases, the primacy index of 2019 is decreasing with respect to the index of 1999, which supports the claim that MCMZ is trending toward a polycentric urban form.

However, despite this evidence of a tendency toward a polycentric urban region, the study also shows two striking trends. First, employment subcenters are concentrating a larger share of jobs in a smaller share of the territory. While in 1999, the 22 employment subcenters concentrated 44.7 percent of the available jobs in 7.3 percent of the city's territory, by 2019, the 29 employment subcenters concentrated 51.9 percent of available jobs in 6.7 percent of the metropolitan

Table 4.6 Employment subcenters' specialization indexes for economic sector and type of job, 2019

Subcenter	*Economic sector*			*Type of jobs*			
	Manufacturing	*Commerce*	*Services*	*Operative*	*Managerial*	*Outsourced*	*Contract*
1. Central Agglomeration	0.21	0.79	1.05	0.90	0.83	0.79	1.14
2. Santa Fe	0.34	0.69	1.45	1.00	1.73	1.34	0.58
3. Naucalpan	3.01	1.65	0.94	1.28	1.11	1.14	0.38
4. Tlalnepantla	2.54	1.71	0.81	1.24	1.03	1.25	0.45
5. Mercado de Abastos	0.55	2.67	0.28	0.88	0.48	0.58	0.36
6. Perisur	0.22	1.07	1.61	0.68	0.76	2.24	3.39
7. Azcapotzalco 1	3.60	1.57	0.51	1.12	1.24	1.37	1.24
8. Aeropuerto	0.00	0.27	0.39	1.16	1.08	1.60	0.09
9. Cuautitlán 1	6.35	0.71	0.50	1.42	1.50	0.80	0.26
10. Benito Juárez/Obregón	1.33	1.29	0.99	1.00	1.12	1.63	0.53
11. Ecatepec 1	5.62	1.14	0.34	1.47	0.84	0.96	0.25
12. Miguel Hidalgo 1	0.35	0.40	0.82	1.22	1.30	0.92	3.24
13. Cuautitlán 2	4.40	1.19	0.13	1.41	1.14	0.95	0.28
14. Iztacalco	5.20	1.89	0.41	1.46	1.10	0.78	0.68
15. Ecatepec 2	3.90	1.45	0.64	1.14	1.13	1.49	0.74
16. Tultitlán 1	3.55	1.24	1.02	1.19	1.14	1.45	0.16
17. Acapotzalco/Cuauhtémoc	4.26	2.05	0.41	1.66	1.22	0.50	0.28
18. Huixquilucan/Cuajimalpa	0.20	1.49	1.83	0.84	1.21	1.10	7.70
19. Ecatepec 3	3.90	0.44	0.15	1.89	0.83	0.44	0.10
20. Miguel Hidalgo 2	0.10	1.36	1.32	1.01	1.04	1.83	0.55
21. Tepotzotlán	3.90	1.18	0.93	1.12	0.89	1.54	0.15
22. Tultitlán 2	4.67	0.25	0.29	1.33	0.96	1.32	0.18
23. Iztapalapa 2	2.75	0.88	0.80	1.33	1.46	0.66	0.30
24. Iztapalapa 3	0.74	1.10	1.82	1.30	1.71	0.73	0.00
25. Texcoco	0.74	2.72	1.14	1.04	0.29	0.54	1.00
26. Tlalpan	0.16	0.79	1.73	0.86	0.99	1.67	0.98
27. Cuauhtémoc/Juárez	3.49	1.68	0.95	1.39	0.53	0.94	0.69
28. Chalco	3.07	1.12	0.32	0.91	0.52	0.53	0.74
29. Gustavo A. Madero	0.00	1.96	0.17	1.03	1.06	1.71	0.82

Source: Author's calculations based on the 2019 Economic Census, National Institute of Statistics, Geography and Informatics (INEGI)

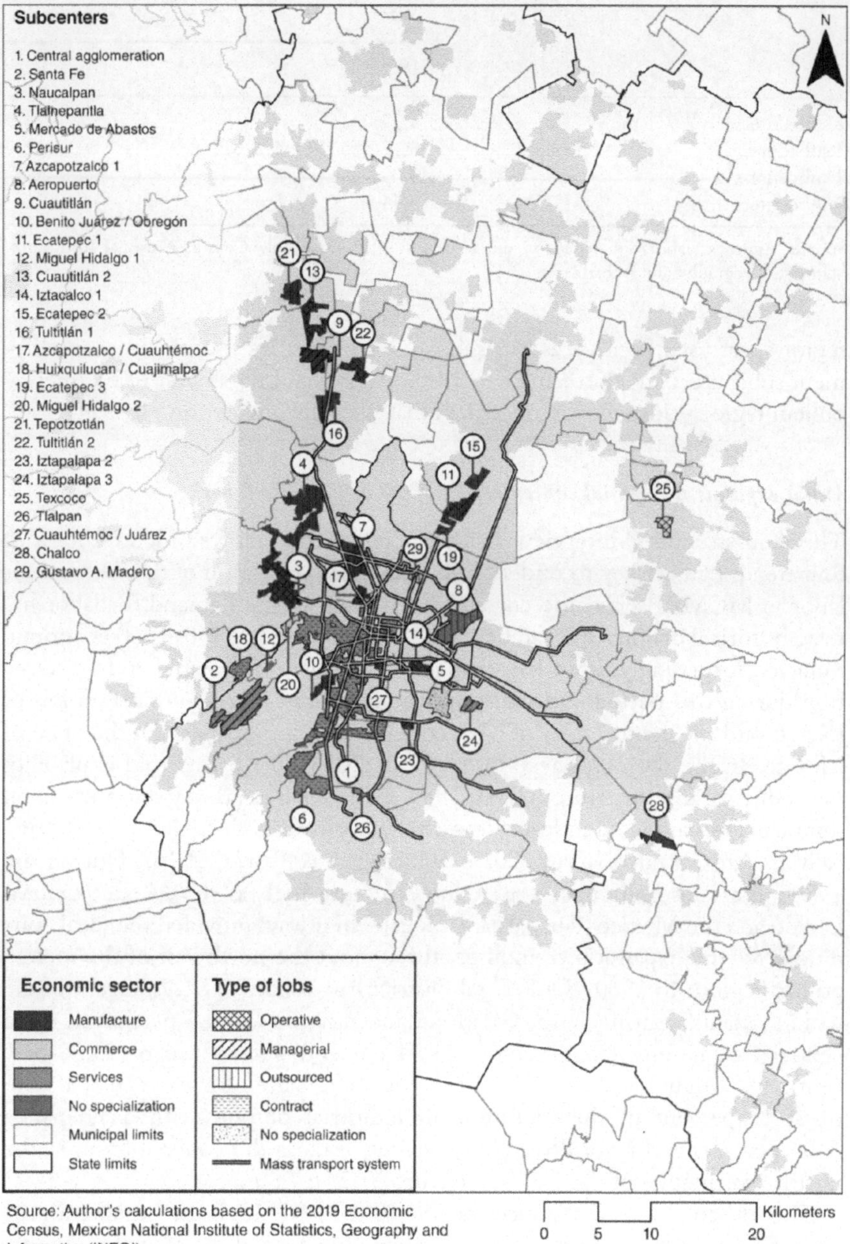

Source: Author's calculations based on the 2019 Economic Census, Mexican National Institute of Statistics, Geography and Informatics (INEGI).

Map 4.4 Employment subcenters, economic specialization, and main type of jobs in MCMZ, 2019

Table 4.7 Primacy indexes for the MCMZ's employment subcenters, 1999 and 2019

	Year	
	1999	2019
2 subcenters	9.37	4.74
3 subcenters	5.17	3.32
4 subcenters	4.09	2.58
5 subcenters	3.44	2.26

Source: Author's elaboration based on the 1999 and 2019 Economic Census, National Institute of Statistics, Geography and Informatics

region's territory. Second, as Maps 4.3 and 4.4 show, most of the new employment subcenters are clustering toward the center and northwest of the metropolitan region, close to the subcenters that were already existing in 1999.

What explains the spatial concentration of the demand for labor?

The semi-structured interviews with key informants allowed identification of four trends that are key to understanding the spatial location of the demand for labor in MCMZ.[5] First, the current distribution of the demand for labor has deep historical origins that can be traced to the Mexican 1940–1960 economic miracle. Surprisingly, little has changed since then. The rapid industrialization during this period laid the foundations for the current concentration of jobs toward the central areas of Mexico City and the northwest of the State of Mexico. In the thorough account of Cruz (2015), the preexisting availability of productive infrastructure (Garza, 1985, 2013) such as railway stations and oil infrastructures attracted industry toward the northwest of Mexico City, specifically in Azcapotzalco (Cruz, 2015; Schteingart & Ibarra, 2016). During the 1950s, the construction of transit infrastructure such as the Mexico-Nuevo Laredo and the Mexico-Guadalajara-Nogales highways provided the ideal conditions for the expansion of industry throughout the northwest of the metropolitan region. In 1960, the Federal District had a share of 81.9 percent of the nation's manufacturing output, with a concentration of 59.3 percent in three central Delegations, Cuauhtémoc (21.94 percent), Azcapotzalco (19.06 percent), and Miguel Hidalgo (18.28 percent). The State of Mexico had a share of 18.12 percent of the metropolitan industrial output, with Tlalnepantla (6.94 percent) and Naucalpan (4.68 percent) leading the concentration in the northwestern zone of the MCMZ (Cruz, 2015, p. 250).

There is consensus that, since the 1980s, the MCMZ is undergoing a process of de-industrialization and a reconfiguration toward the service economy (Carrillo & Cadena, 2019; Cruz, 2015; Garza, 2000, 2006, 2011). Researchers have made important efforts to understand how this economic reconfiguration is changing the urban form of MCMZ. During the 1940–1960 Mexican economic miracle, the MCMZ showed a monocentric urban form with

83.8 percent of the service economy located within three central delegations (Garza, 2020). Research shows that the spatial patterns of the service economy started their transition toward a polycentric urban form between the 1960s and the 1980s (Garza, 2011, 2020). This trend continued, and by 2019, the new employment subcenters with an economic specialization in the service sector are located toward the south (Perisur and Tlalpan) and west (Santa Fe) of Mexico City (Map 4.4). Eastern-MCMZ has failed to ride the wave of economic reconfiguration and has not been able to produce any service sector employment subcenter.

Second, another explanation focuses on the institutional arrangements that determine land-use patterns. According to some of the interviewees, current land-use regulation in Eastern-MCMZ scares away private investment, as most land regulation in this area allows only for residential use or low-impact economic activity. Manufacturing or high-density land uses are not an option that is allowed by land-use regulation. As a byproduct of these institutional constraints on land use, when inhabitants of Eastern-MCMZ want to use their land for economic activities in manufacturing, they must do so informally. Interviewees provided plenty illustrations of informal manufacturing taking place in Nezahualcoyotl.

While these underground manufacturing activities create a considerable number of jobs, these informal jobs are not accounted for in official statistics. Additionally, this mismatch between the kind of economic activity in which the population participates in, and the land-use regulation in Eastern-MCMZ hinders the productive capacity of the subregion in important ways. The productive capacity of informal manufacturing firms is capped by infrastructure deficiencies (Lee et al., 1999). Land-use regulation prevents manufacturing firms from having larger production floors or from introducing key energy or logistics infrastructures needed to scale-up their operations. Operating informally, manufacturing firms are unable to access the legal status that would allow them to expand their markets by participating in larger productive chains. When manufacturing firms do want to scale-up their operation or participate in larger-scale production chains, they must leave Eastern-MCMZ and move to an alternate location with more permissive land-use regulation and adequate infrastructure.

Third, in addition to these institutional constraints on land use, there seems to be a symbolic dimension to the geographies that are associated with entrepreneurial success. Interviewees described how certain areas of the metropolitan region have established images as symbols of entrepreneurial success, such as Roma, Condesa, Polando, Interlomas, or Santa Fe. Conversely, Eastern-MCMZ fails to be perceived by entrepreneurs as a location that conveys success. This symbolic understanding of entrepreneurial success operates as a centripetal force that pulls private productive investment toward preexisting employment subcenters.

Fourth, many interviewees agreed on the contribution of state-led economic development projects in creating employment subcenters. The most cited case was Santa Fe, a megaproject spearheaded by the Mexico City Government in the 1990s with the goals of attracting global capital and consolidating Mexico City as a global city (Moreno, 2008; Pérez, 2012). Although its location produced considerable transportation problems and political conflicts over transport infrastructure (Sosa, 2017), the project was successful enough that Santa Fe moved in the urban hierarchy from the eleventh employment subcenter in 1999 to the second by 2019. For interviewees, state-led megaprojects have shown their potential to generate new employment subcenters.

Conclusions

This chapter conducted an empirical analysis to assess the trends in the spatial location of the demand for labor in the MCMZ between 1999 and 2019. The chapter also identified some of the key urban policies and factors that have driven such trends. One of the main findings of the study is that despite the MCMZ increasing its absolute number of employment subcenters (from 22 in 1999 to 29 in 2019), and showing a primacy index trend toward a polycentric urban form (from 3.44 in 1999 to 2.26 in 2019), by other key measures, employment keeps concentrating in space. In 1999, 52.8 percent of the jobs available in the metropolitan region were concentrated in 9.3 of its territory, while by 2019, 58.5 percent of the jobs were concentrated in 8.4 percent of the territory. Furthermore, most of the new employment subcenters and most of those moving up in the urban hierarchy are in the center, west, and northwest of the metropolitan region.

The Eastern-MCMZ has failed to attract jobs. While two new employment subcenters appeared in Eastern-MCMZ in 2019 (Texcoco and Chalco), these occupy the lowest tier in the urban hierarchy (25 and 28, respectively). This trend in the geography of jobs puts the population residing in the Eastern-MCMZ at a considerable disadvantage with respect to the population located closer to the main employment subcenters. This is especially true for workers participating in the manufacturing or service sector. Almost all the employment subcenters with an economic specialization in manufacturing are located in the industrial corridor situated at the northwest of the MCMZ. Most of the employment subcenters in the service sector are in the Central Agglomeration or in the emerging subcenters of Santa Fe (in the west) or Perisur (in the south). This is problematic because accessing the jobs located in these employment subcenters comes at a high commuting cost for residents of Eastern-MCMZ.

Notes

1 Following Garrocho and Campos (2007, p. 118), the local specialization indexes are calculated by relating the percentage of employment in each economic sector (manufacturing, commerce, and service) with respect to the total employment in each subcenter, with the percentage of employment in each economic sector with respect to the total employment in all the subcenters of the city. The following formula is used:

$$EI_s = (E_{s,\ i}/E_{s,\ t})/(ESM_{,\ i}/ESM_{,\ t})$$

were:

IEs = Local Specialization Index of subcenter s
Es, i = Employment of subcenter s in sector i
Es, t = Total employment in subcenter i
ESM, i = Employment in subcenters of MCMZ in sector i
ESM, t = Total employments of subcenters in MCMZ

The values of the local specialization index below "1" indicate that there is no specialization. The values above "1" correspond to the sectors that show specialization with respect to the other subcenters. The values in the index express the "intensity" of the local specialization, as they represent the difference in the proportion of employment in sector i in subcenter s, with respect to the proportion of employment in the same sector i at the scale of the employment subcenters as a whole.

2 The primacy index is useful to measure the extent to which a metropolitan area is trending toward a monocentric or a polycentric urban form. The index measures the predominance of the main employment subcenter over the rest of the city's employment subcenters. Such predominance is measured by evaluating the relative size of the larger employment subcenter in relation to the next ranked subcenters in the hierarchy. Growth in the primacy index from one point in time to the other will indicate that the city is trending toward a monocentric urban form. A decrease of the index will show that the city is trending toward polycentrism. Some authors calculate the primacy index by comparing the biggest employment subcenter with the next three subcenters in the hierarchy (Plata, 2012), while other authors compare it to the next four (Garrocho & Campos, 2007). Some authors calculate several primacy indexes for two, three, four, and five subcenters to assess different scenarios (Unikel et al., 1976). I take the latter approach.

3 This table corresponds with Maps 4.1 and 4.2.

4 The inspiration to call this employment subcenter the "Central Agglomeration" comes from Suárez and Delgado (2009), who in their article published in *Urban Studies* proposed this name for this employment subcenter.

5 As described in the introductory chapter of this book, the investigation of the political economy of the demand for labor in MCMZ is based on semi-structured interviews with 34 key informants coming from urban development and mobility experts, government officials, civil society organizations, and academia.

References

Aguilar, A., & Hernández, J. (2012). Transformación metropolitana y estructura policéntrica en la Ciudad de México. Identificación de subcentros urbanos, 1990–2005. In A. Ziccardi (Ed.), *Ciudades del 2010: Entre la sociedad del conocimiento y la desigualdad social*. Ciudad de México: Universidad Nacional Autónoma de México.

Baerwald, T. J. (1982). Land use change in suburban clusters and corridors. *Transportation Research Record, 891*, 7–12.

Baumont, C., Ertur, C., & Le Gallo, J. (2004). Spatial analysis of employment and population density: The case of the agglomeration of Dijon 1999. *Geographical Analysis, 36*(2), 146–176.

Bourne, L. S. (1989). Are new urban forms emerging? Empirical tests for Canadian urban areas. *The Canadian Geographer, 33*(4), 312–328.

Carrillo, B., & Cadena, E. (2019). Terciarización y configuración espacial en México Tertiarization and spatial configuration in Mexico Resumen. *Acta Universitaria, 29*, 1–21.

Cervero, R. (1989). *America's suburban centers: The land use – transportation link*. Sidney: Unwin Hyman.

Cervero, R., & Wu, K. (1997). Polycentrism, commuting, and residential location in the San Francisco Bay area. *Environment and Planning A: Economy and Space, 29*(5), 865–886.

Clark, W., & Kuijpers-Linde, M. (1994). Commuting in restructuring urban regions. *Urban Studies, 31*(3), 465–483.

Craig, S. G., & Ng, P. T. (2001). Using quantile smoothing splines to identify employment subcenters in a multicentric urban area. *Journal of Urban Economics, 49*(1), 100–120.

Cruz, F. (2015). *Configuración espacial de la industria en la Ciudad de México*. Ciudad de México: El Colegio de México.

Erickson, R. A. (1986). Multinucleation in metropolitan economies. *Annals of the Association of American Geographers, 76*(3), 331–346.

García, M. Á., & Muñiz, I. (2005). *Descentralización del empleo: ¿Compactación policéntrica o dispersión? El caso de la Región Metropolitana de Barcelona 1986–1996. Departament d'Economia Aplicada*. Universidad Autónoma de Barcelona.

Garrocho, C., & Campos, J. (2007). Dinámica de la estructura policéntrica del empleo terciario en el Área Metropolitana de Toluca, 1994–2004. *Papeles de Población, 52*, 110–135.

Garza, G. (1985). *El proceso de Industrialización de la Ciudad de México, 1821-1970*. Ciudad de México: El Colegio de México.

Garza, G. (2000). Superconcentración, crisis y globalización del sector industrial, 1930–1998. In G. Garza (Ed.), *La Ciudad de México en el fin del segundo milenio*. Ciudad de México: El Colegio de México, Gobierno del Distrito Federal.

Garza, G. (2006). *La organización espacial del sector servicios en México*. Ciudad de México: El Colegio de México.

Garza, G. (2011). *Visión comprensiva de la distribución territorial del sector servicios en México*. Ciudad de México: El Colegio de México.

Garza, G. (2013). *Teoría de las condiciones y los servicios generales de la producción*. Ciudad de México: El Colegio de México.

Garza, G. (2020). *Economía política de la estructuración del comercio y los servicios en la Ciudad de México*. Ciudad de México: ePromethium Ediciones Digitales.

Giuliano, G., & Small, K. A. (1991). Subcenters in the Los Angeles region. *Regional Science and Urban Economics, 21*(2), 163–182.

Gordon, P., & Richardson, H. (1996). Beyond polycentricity. The dispersed metropolis, Los Angeles, 1970–1990. *Journal of the American Planning Association, 62*(3), 289–295.

Gordon, P., Richardson, H., & Wong, H. (1986). The distribution of population and employment in a polycentric city: The case of Los Angeles. *Environment and Planning A, 18*(2), 161–173.

Green, D. L. (1980). Recent trends in urban spatial structure. *Growth and Change, 11*, 29–40.

Guillain, R., Le Gallo, J., & Boiteux-Orain, C. (2004). *The evolution of the spatial and sectoral patterns in Ile-De-France over 1978–1997*. Louvain-la-Neuve: ERSA Conference Papers.

Lee, K. S., Anas, A., & Oh, G. T. (1999). Costs of infrastructure deficiencies for manufacturing in Nigerian, Indonesian and Thai cities. *Urban Studies, 36*(12), 2135–2149.

López-García, D., & Gómez-Álvarez, D. (2022). Estructura Urbana del Área Metropolitana de Guadalajara, 1999–2014: Un Análisis de Subcentros de Empleo. *Estudios Demográficos y Urbanos, 37*(2), 427–481.

McDonald, J. (1987). The identification of urban employment subcenters. *Journal of Urban Economics, 21*(2), 242–258.

McDonald, J., & McMillen, D. (1990). Employment subcenters and land values in a polycentric urban areas: The case of Chicago. *Environment and Planning A: Economy and Space, 22*(12), 1561–1574.

McDonald, J., & Prather, P. (1994). Suburban employment centres: The case of Chicago. *Urban Studies, 31*(2), 201–218.

McMillen, D. (2001). Nonparametric employment subcenter identification. *Journal of Urban Economics, 50*(3), 448–473.

McMillen, D. (2003). The return of centralization to Chicago: Using repeat sales to identify changes in house price distance gradients. *Regional Science and Urban Economics, 33*(3), 287–304.

McMillen, D., & McDonald, J. (1997). A nonparametric analysis of employment density in a polycentric city. *Journal of Regional Science, 37*(4), 591–612.

McMillen, D., & Smith, S. (2003). The number of subcenters in large urban areas. *Journal of Urban Economics, 53*(3), 321–338.

Montejano, J., Caudillo, C., & Silván, J. (2016). Contesting Mexico City's alleged polycentric condition through a centrality-mixed land-use composite index. *Urban Studies, 53*(11), 2380–2396.

Moreno, M. (2008). La producción espacial de lo global: lo público y lo privado en Santa Fe, Ciudad de México. *Alteridades, 18*(36), 75–86.

Muñiz, I., Galindo, A., & García, M. Á. (2003). *¿Es Barcelona una ciudad policéntrica? Departament d'Economia Aplicada*. Barcelona: Universidad Autónoma de Barcelona.

Pérez, M. (2012). Santa Fe como una nueva forma de producción del espacio urbano. In E. Duhau (Ed.), *Ciudad de México: La construcción permanente de la metrópoli*. Quito: OLACCHI.

Plata, J. A. (2012). Estimaciones de la Población e Índice de Primacía de las Ciudades Principales de Honduras, 2001–2015. *Población y Desarrollo – Argonautas y Caminantes, 8*, 95–103.

Roy, A., & AlSayyad, N. (2003). *Urban informality. Transnational perspectives from Middle East, Latin America, and South Asia*. Oxford: Lexington Books.

Schteingart, M., & Ibarra, V. (2016). *Desarrollo urbano-ambiental y movilidad en la Ciudad de México: Evaluación histórica, cambios recientes y políticas públicas*. Ciudad de México: El Colegio de México.

Sosa, O. (2017). Urban mobility and politics in Mexico City. *Latin American Perspectives, 44*(2), 184–204.

Suárez, M., & Delgado, J. (2009). Is Mexico City polycentric? A trip attaction capacity approach. *Urban Studies, 46*(10), 2187–2211.

Unikel, L., Riuz, C., & Garza, G. (1976). *El desarrollo urbano de México. Diagnóstico e implicaciones futuras*. Ciudad de México: El Colegio de México.

Ward, P. M. (2019). Learning from Latin America's Informal Sector. *Latin American Research Review, 54*(1), 277–285.

5 Housing pathways and the mobility experience of workers

In the previous chapter, I argued that to really understand what shapes the mobility experience of workers, one needs to consider the relationship between the availability of transport systems and the spatial distribution of origins and destinations. I then explored the destinations by presenting a study of employment subcenters in MCMZ. I will now deal with the origins of trips: the residential location of workers. The mainstream model about location decisions assumes that households decide their residential location by participating in housing markets with perfect information, without coercion, and with freedom of choice. It is also assumed that residential land closer to employment subcenters is more expensive than land further away and that transportation costs rise with increased distance between the residence and employment subcenters. Under these assumptions, households must navigate their location decisions by accepting an unescapable trade-off between housing and commuting costs.[1]

According to this mainstream model, locating closer to employment subcenters reduces transportation costs, but households must pay more for housing and consume a smaller number of square meters. Conversely, locating further away from employment subcenters reduces the cost of housing, allowing for the consumption of more square meters, but increases transportation costs. Households then shop around the housing market and decide on the residential location that provides them with an equilibrium between their housing and transportation costs. When aggregated, the model argues, the individual decision of thousands of households brings the housing market to a happy general equilibrium where every household assumes the transportation costs that they are willing to pay.

But there is so much more about residential location decisions that the mainstream model is not able to capture and that undermine the freedom of choice assumption, especially in cities of the Global South. Land-use and housing policies can influence both the demand and the supply side of housing markets, thus limiting the options available for households. Housing developers must navigate the institutional arrangements produced by land-use and housing policies to use urban space—a key input in housing production—most profitably. In the Global South, this often means building the high-end housing units closer to employment subcenters and affordable housing in the urban

DOI: 10.4324/9781003261698-5

periphery. As per the demand side, affordable housing options subsidized by housing policy are often available only in peripheral areas. Workers who qualify for housing policies have no option but to locate in the urban fringe. Furthermore, many households simply refuse to participate in housing markets, satisfying their housing needs by building their housing unit through their own means on whatever land they can get a hold. In short, it is false that workers have freedom of choice to navigate housing markets and make location decisions. Workers are by and large bounded by preexisting default options from which they cannot escape.

This chapter argues that housing policies and default housing choices partially determine the mobility experience of workers. The case of Eastern-MCMZ is analyzed, a subregion with a well-deserved reputation of being a dormitory city that lacks enough jobs for its inhabitants (Hiernaux & Lindón, 2004; Quiroz, 2013). To build this argument, I investigate why workers in Eastern-MCMZ live in a geography of low accessibility to jobs in the first place. I resort to the analytical lens of housing pathways (Clapham, 2002), which allows the study of the housing decisions and routes of households and individuals. Based on semi-structured interviews and focus groups with residents of the area of study, the chapter identifies three distinct ideal types of relationships between housing pathways and workers' mobility experiences: *housing use value-based*, *national housing policy-based*, and *access to labor market-based*. The study shows a relationship between the types of jobs that workers have access to, the housing pathways available for them, and their mobility experience.

Analytical strategy and research methods

The concept of *housing pathways* was put forward by Clapham (2002) as an analytical strategy to study the housing routes that households and individuals take over time (Hamzah & Zyed, 2021). Defined as "patterns of interaction (practices) concerning housing and home, over time and space" (Clapham, 2002, p. 63), housing pathways studies the individual steps through which households and individuals manage to gain access to housing (Hochstenbach & Boterman, 2015). The housing pathways analytical framework accounts for the structure and context in which housing decisions are made, the agency of households and individuals to move along available pathways, and the interaction between the two (Wiesel, 2014). The approach assumes that the process of housing acquisition is a tactically and strategically planned process (Deng et al., 2020; Hochstenbach & Boterman, 2015) by which households and individuals adapt their housing decisions in response to the changing context and the situations they face (Clapham et al., 2014). The housing pathways framework assumes that the housing routes are related to other pathways such as employment or family maturation (Clapham, 2003), and by individual circumstances in terms of resources (Clapham et al., 2014).

Assuming that certain typical housing pathways can be identified and generalized from individual housing practices (Clapham, 2002, 2005; Hochstenbach &

Boterman, 2015), the empirical investigation of housing pathways entails the documentation of individual housing experiences aiming to identify salient patterns or typologies (Deng et al., 2020). In terms of data collection methods, researchers resort to qualitative methods to identify how households and individuals navigate their context and specific circumstances in their housing moves (Deng et al., 2020). The housing pathways approach has been successfully applied to the study of housing decisions in urban settings from China (Deng et al., 2020), Malaysia (Hamzah & Zyed, 2021), the Netherlands (Hochstenbach & Boterman, 2015), Australia (Wiesel, 2014), and England (Clapham et al., 2014), among other places.

While the study of housing pathways has traditionally focused on the study of households and their strategies, less attention has been put in the literature to the study of the context within which housing decisions are made (Clapham et al., 2014). Aiming to narrow this gap in the literature, this chapter furthers the study of the context within which housing pathways take place by resorting to the *housing forms of production* framework. Put forward by Jaramillo (1981, 1982), and further developed in Jaramillo and Schteingart (1983), Schteingart (1983, 1989), and Jaramillo (1985), the categories of analysis in the housing forms of production framework bring helpful analytical lenses for the study of housing in Latin American cities and in the Global South in general.

The forms of housing production framework holds that capitalist economies are characterized by the coexistence of several forms or systems for the production and circulation of housing (Schteingart, 1983) called *forms of production* (Bettelheim, 1976; Jaramillo, 1981, 1982). The neo-Marxist concept of forms of production is defined as a system of relations in which there are distinct assigned roles for the agents that participate in the production and circulation of goods (Jaramillo, 1985; Schteingart, 1983). Specifically, Jaramillo (1985) proposes identifying the following roles. *Direct labor*, which is the mobilization of human labor force in the construction of housing. *Technical control of production*, the capacity to coordinate the operation of the means of production involved in housing construction. That is, coordinating the labor force, the inputs for production, and the techniques used. *Direct economic control of production* is having control over the economic aspects of housing production. This means having the capacity to start the productive process, define its characteristics, and determine the availability of the product. Finally, *indirect economic control of production* entails the capacity to affect production from outside the productive process. This means having control over the context within which agents that exert direct economic control operate.

Building on these distinct roles, the framework puts forward that Latin American housing is composed of four main types of housing production forms (Jaramillo, 1985; Schteingart, 1983, 1989). The first is called *self-construction*, in which the consumer of housing is at the same time the direct producer, provides the labor, and keeps technical and direct economic control over the production process (Jaramillo, 1985). The second is called *production by commission* (producción por encargo, in Spanish), in which the final user of the housing unit hires an agent specialized in construction. The final user is the owner of the land and therefore keeps the direct economic control (Jaramillo, 1985). The agent hired to do the construction keeps the technical control over production and manages labor. The housing stock produced both by self-construction and by production by commission is not initially intended to go out on the market, and its motivation is not generating profit, but to alleviate people's housing needs. While self-construction is a strategy commonly used by the low-income population, production by commission is used by population from all income strata. It is often the case that the middle- and high-income population resort to production by commission without any credit or any type of governmental support. They would just hire contractors to build their housing unit. The low-income population, however, can resort to a mix of forms of housing production by which they self-build most of the housing unit but hire specialists such as plumbers or electricians to do the most specialized and technical aspects of the construction.

The third housing production form is called *private developer production* (promoción promocional privada, in Spanish), in which the agent with direct economic control over production is a capitalist (Schteingart, 1983). The agent with technical control of production is a capitalist as well. In this case, housing production is motivated by capital accumulation via the rent produced by labor and land speculation (Schteingart, 1989). The fourth is called *state promotion* (producción promocional del Estado, in Spanish), which occurs when the state resorts to policy instruments to secure the production of housing (Jaramillo, 1985). This can take several forms. For instance, sometimes the state can have direct economic and technical control over production, building in state-owned land, and financing operations (Schteingart, 1989). Other times, the state can provide the capital for capitalist agents to engage in private developer production or for consumers to purchase housing units (Jaramillo, 1985).[2]

Two aspects should be kept in mind when applying the housing forms of production framework. The first is that the development of each of these forms of production does not occur independently from each other. Instead, housing forms of production are interrelated and compete between them, which in turn affects their expansion, retreat, and the domination of one over the other (Schteingart, 1989). In the Global South, self-construction and production by commission are two widespread forms through which low-income populations have traditionally pursued their housing needs, but advanced for-profit forms of production have consistently won terrain and developed. Second, public policy plays a key role in the trajectory of forms of housing production by supporting the operation of developers and facilitating housing consumption (Jaramillo & Schteingart, 1983). For instance, governments can support for-profit developers by providing capital for construction, changing land use, or enacting institutional arrangements that favor their operation, among other policies. Governments can also support the demand side by providing funds for purchasing a housing unit or upgrading an existing one, subsidizing the cost of housing units, legalizing land, or providing basic public services, among other strategies.

Building on these analytical lenses, this chapter explores the housing pathways available for workers of Eastern-MCMZ in the context of existing housing forms of production.[3] The findings are based on the analysis of semi-structured interviews with 25 residents from the area of study conducted during the Fall of 2018, and March, June, and July of 2019. The sample selection for the interviews consisted of a snowball strategy, through which participants in the study recommended other potential participants until a point of saturation was reached. Four focus groups were organized with the support of some interview participants, who volunteered to support the research project by inviting neighbors to a session. The focus groups were organized in the mayoralty of Iztapalapa in Mexico City, and the municipalities of Nezahualcóyotl, Chimalhuacán, and Ixtapaluca in the State of Mexico.

Interviews and focus groups were audio-recorded and put into a transcription that was later analyzed through a memoing strategy. Such strategy consists of reading the transcript and making a memo every time interviewees and focus group participants touch upon any of the categories of analysis of the analytical framework. When memoing, special attention was put in characterizing the relationship between housing forms of production, housing pathways, and the mobility experience of workers.

Research findings

The semi-structured interviews with residents of the area of study allowed to identify three distinct ideal types of relationships between housing pathways and the mobility experience of workers. The first ideal type is called *housing use value-based* and relates to housing forms of production such as self-construction and production by commission. The second ideal type is called *housing exchange value-based* and is related with the private developer and the state promotion housing forms of production. The third ideal type is called *access to labor market-based* and is not related with housing forms of production *per se*, but with the success of workers in achieving access to better paying labor markets. Each of these ideal types is composed, in turn, of specific subtypes of relationships between housing pathways and mobility experiences, which I will now explain in detail.

Mobility experience based on the use value of housing

The first ideal type of relationship between housing pathways and the mobility experience of workers is based on housing forms of production related to the *use value* of housing (Figure 5.1). In this ideal type, workers access housing either through self-construction, production by commission, or a combination of both, and do not resort to private developers or state promotions. This ideal type has its origins in the Mexican economic miracle that took place between 1940 and 1960. The accelerated concentration of industrial activity in the MCMZ came hand in hand with rapid urbanization. During 1940–1960,

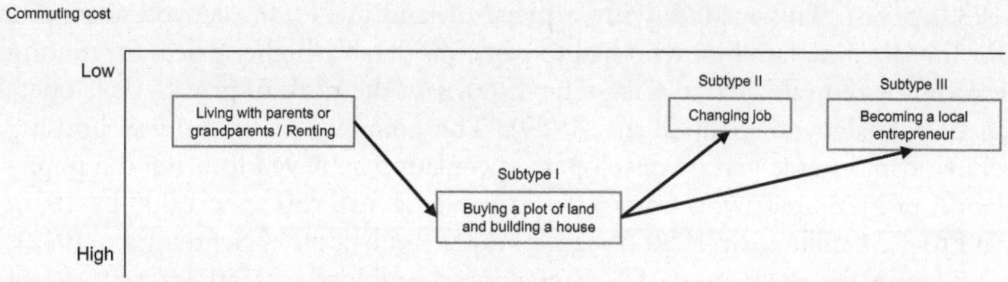

Figure 5.1 Mobility experience based on the use value of housing

Mexico City attracted important waves of migration from the rest of the country. These migrants would usually locate near the emerging industrial agglomerations in the central delegations of Mexico City, and in the northeast of the State of Mexico (Cruz, 2015). In general, the population that arrived at Mexico City during this period was engaged in secondary and informal labor markets that lack access to the existing social safety net. This meant that this population had no access to the national housing policy, which, as will be explained next, is linked to having a formal job.

Driven by the desire to improve their living conditions, the migrant workers of the 1950s and 1960s were determined to own a housing unit. This longing coupled with one of the first housing policies that would expel Mexico City's population toward the State of Mexico: the prohibition of *Regente* Uruchurtu (the equivalent of the Mexico City's Mayor) in 1964 to build new housing units within Mexico City's political boundaries (Castillo, 2010). The longing to own their housing unit, and the restrictions for new construction within Mexico City, made the migrant workers look for new possibilities in the neighboring State of Mexico. One of the most important alternatives had been brewing for years and was ready to be seized: Nezahualcoyotl. An account of Nezahualcoyotl urbanization is beyond the scope of this chapter.[4] Suffice to say that during the 1940s, private developers were able to attain the historically contested property rights of the new land that emerged as a byproduct of the Texcoco lake desiccation at the east of Mexico City, in the State of Mexico. During the 1950s, private developers maneuvered to subdivide the land into approximately 150 thousand plots of land of approximately 150 square meters each and sell them to the low-income population of Mexico City without any kind of infrastructure or public services (Schteingart, 1989). The population would then maintain technical and economic control over the production of their housing units either through self-construction, construction by commission, or a combination.

According to the interviewees, buying land in Nezahualcoyotl was the only feasible housing pathway for the urban poor who lacked access to any kind of formal housing credit, as developers would grant them credit based solely on their word (known as *crédito a la palabra*, in Spanish). The monthly payment for a plot of land represented only 3 percent of the minimum wage (Schteingart, 1989, p. 88). This made buying a piece of land in Nezahualcoyotl accessible for low-income families, who had to pay considerably higher prices for renting a room in central Mexico City. The 1960s saw the peak of private developers in Nezahualcoyotl (Schteingart, 1989). The coupling of the intense housing demand and fierce private developers' speculation achieved to bring the population of Nezahualcoyotl from 6,000 inhabitants in 1950 to 651,000 by 1970, and to 1.34 million by 1980 (Negrete, 2000; Rubalcava & Schteingart, 2012). Over time, the population of Nezahualcoyotl unfolded into other territories of Eastern-MCMZ. By replicating housing pathways related to the use value of housing, the second and third generations of Nezahualcoyotl's population have located further into Eastern-MCMZ in municipalities such as Chimalhuacán or Los Reyes. This urbanization and residential location pattern kept pushing the population into the urban periphery and further away from the MCMZ's employment subcenters.

Workers moving into their new housing units but keeping their jobs unchanged led to the commuting experience depicted in Figure 5.1 as subtype I. In this subtype of commuting experience, workers are further away from the places where their jobs are located, therefore having a more costly commute. The increasing commuting cost of subtype I was sometimes faced by dropping the jobs located in central areas and making a living through a couple of distinct strategies. In the first strategy, some opted for getting a new job closer to their places of residence in peripheral areas. Such jobs would usually be low-paid and without benefits, as most of the economic activities in peripheral areas are informal and in low-productivity sectors. This strategy produced the commuting experience depicted as subtype II. In the second strategy, some decided to become local entrepreneurs by opening businesses catering for the needs of the growing population. By establishing pharmacies, groceries, furniture, hardware stores, and the like, many made a successful career as business owners. This strategy produced the commuting experience presented in Figure 5.1 as subtype III. In both subtypes II and III, the population managed to lower their commuting costs and therefore achieved a more pleasant mobility experience.

Mobility experience based on the national housing policy

The second ideal type is based on housing forms of production related to the national housing policy (Figure 5.2). In this housing pathway, private developers produce affordable housing units for a profit while the state implemented policy instruments aiming both to support the production of housing stock by developers and to subsidize workers' housing ownership. Technical control of housing production remained in the hands of private developers. Economic control was shared by both the private developers and the state, as the latter developed and implemented an array of institutional and financial policy instruments to foster housing production and consumption.

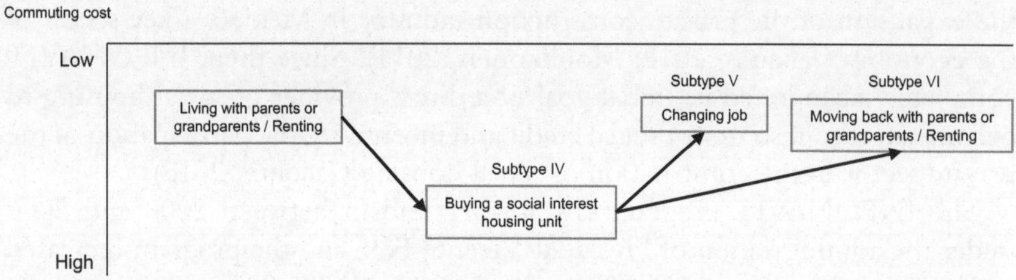

Figure 5.2 Mobility experience based on the national housing policy

Having access to the Mexican national housing policy is linked to participating in formal labor markets. The origins of this link can be traced to the Mexican economic miracle of 1940–1960. During the 1940s, the Mexican Federal Government used social policy as a way to assemble an urban coalition that pushed to modernize the country via imports substitution and industrialization (Barba & Valencia, 2013). The central institution of this process was the social safety net linked to formal jobs. Such institutional arrangements have produced a dual safety net system that has generated institutional segmentation. While the formal urban workers (usually industrial), government employees, and the armed forces enjoyed access to the social safety net, informal urban workers, rural residents, indigenous, and Afro-descendant population were by and large left outside of the safety net. Among the institutions designed within the safety net, there are the pensions system, the health care system, the public education system, the childcare system, and the *national housing policy*. In terms of housing, the social safety net materialized in the creation of the National Workers' Housing Fund and the State Employees' Housing Fund (INFONAVIT and FOVISSSTE, by their acronyms in Spanish, respectively), created both in 1972, and the Military Housing Fund (FOVIMI, by its acronym in Spanish) created in 1973 (Barba & Valencia, 2013).

Since its creation in 1972, INFONAVIT has been the most important venue offered to the public within the national housing policy pathway by being the program with the largest number of contributors and therefore having the largest budget (García, 2010). The program has seen a series of reforms that have produced different outcomes throughout time. In its early years, INFONAVIT built and promoted housing units directly. The units financed by direct provision comprised 88 percent of the total units built by INFONAVIT in 1974–1975 but decreased to 3.15 percent by 1979, and ceased completely in 1980 (Schteingart, 1989). As a consequence of reduced revenues, increased construction costs, and an unsustainable lending policy with interest rates far below the market rate and almost no legal recourse to secure collection, by the late 1980s, the program was almost bankrupt (Monkkonen, 2011). The program saw important reforms in 1992 and 1997 to pursue two goals: first, transforming INFONAVIT into a bank-like system with the aim of lending as much as possible and earning a return on investment, and second, to foster the expansion of the private construction industry in Mexico, a key sector of the economy (Jacquin, 2012; Monkkonen, 2011). Since then, INFONAVIT completely abandoned its initial goal of a direct provider of social housing to become an administrator of social credit and incentivize the participation of the private sector in the construction of social housing (Jacquin, 2012).

The INFONAVIT program saw further reform between 2000 and 2006 under the administration of President Vicente Fox, and the program increased its lending volume from 230,000 credits in 2001 to 420,000 in 2006 (Monkkonen, 2011). The increase of INFONAVIT lending was coupled with a central area re-densification policy called *Bando 2*, implemented by the then Mexico City Mayor Andres Manuel López-Obrador. The *Bando 2* was a land-use policy implemented between 2000 and 2005 that prohibited new construction of housing units in Mexico City except for the four central delegations: Miguel Hidalgo, Cuauhtémoc, Venustiano Carranza, and Benito Juárez. Given the decrease in the supply of land for new construction within Mexico City, one of the well-documented effects of the Bando 2 policy was to increase land values in the four central delegations in which new construction was still legal. Consequently, new construction in the central delegations was oriented toward high-end expensive housing. As a result, the construction of social housing through the INFONAVIT program shifted into the MCMZ peripheral zones where land was available and cheap (Arenales & Esquivel, 2012; Flores & Bornazou, 2012; Jacquin, 2012). This sparked an intense process of urban sprawl towards the periphery. By the year 2011, it was calculated that 15 percent of the MCMZ population (approximately three million people) lived in this type of social housing development (Jacquin, 2012). In Eastern-MCMZ, thousands of housing units linked to the INFONAVIT program were constructed in the municipalities of Ixtapaluca and Chicoloapan.

The intense relocation of workers into Eastern-MCMZ via the national housing policy has produced the mobility experience depicted Figure 5.2 as subtype IV. This is a mobility experience in which the journey to work needs more distance and demands more time. The mechanism through which this occurs is as follows. Workers have access to the national housing policy because they have a formal job. But most formal jobs are in the metropolitan region's employment subcenters. As seen in Chapter 3, most of the employment subcenters in the MCMZ are in the central and northwestern areas of the metropolitan region. As access to the Mexican social safety net depends on having a formal job, the newcomers into Eastern-MCMZ cannot change into an informal job located nearer their new residential location; they cannot go into self-employment or engage in entrepreneurial activities. Workers are then forced to commute from their new residential location in Eastern-MCMZ to their formal jobs typically located in employment subcenters.

Interviewees did report, however, on a couple of strategies through which they have achieved a more pleasant mobility experience. In the first, some interviewees managed to change into a formal job located nearer their place of residence. This change in the location of their jobs produces the mobility experience depicted in Figure 5.2 as subtype V. Nevertheless, for inhabitants of Eastern-MCMZ, this strategy is difficult to implement given that most of the available formal jobs are in the center, west, and northwest of the metropolitan region (see Chapter 3). A second strategy reported by interviewees consists of moving away from the housing unit acquired through the national housing policy and moving back into their parents' or grandparents' housing units or renting closer to the location of their jobs. The motivations for this move vary. Sometimes, the mobility experience of interviewees became so extenuating that they could simply not live through it anymore. Other times, interviewees wait until their children reach higher education age and, as most of universities are in central areas, they move away from peripheral areas and closer to their kids' universities and employment subcenters. This strategy leads to the mobility experience presented in Figure 5.2 as subtype VI. In both subtypes V and VI, workers are able to move closer to the location of their jobs, therefore achieving a more pleasant mobility experience.

Mobility experience based on access to primary labor markets

The third ideal type of mobility experience of workers is not related to housing pathways per se but to increasing human capital in Eastern-MCMZ and increased access to better, but more distant, labor markets (Figure 5.3). As generations go by, the Eastern-MCMZ population is achieving higher educational attainment. A skill mismatch is then being produced. Available jobs in Eastern-MCMZ are not a good match for the increasing human capital of its workforce. Job opportunities in Eastern-MCMZ are low-paid jobs better suited for unskilled workers. Furthermore, they are often informal jobs that lack any social safety net. Having no matching job alternatives within Eastern-MCMZ and, should the Eastern-MCMZ workers aspire to get a job that pays in accordance with their increased educational attainment, they must look for job opportunities in the main employment subcenters. This, in turn, increases the physical separation between residential locations and jobs and therefore produces a costly mobility experience. In this case, access to better labor markets produces the mobility experience depicted in Figure 5.3 as subtype VII.

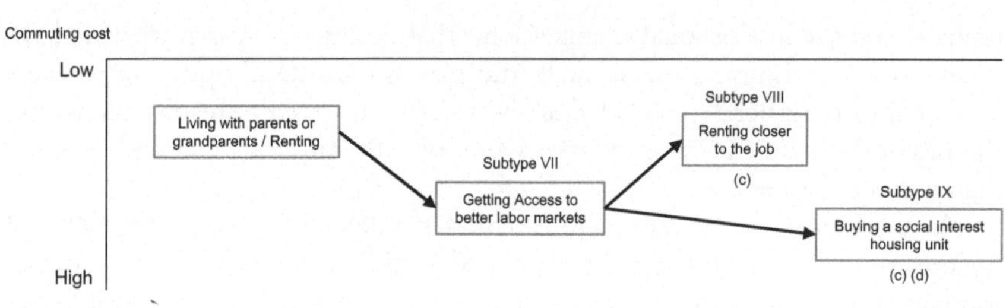

Figure 5.3 Mobility experience based on access to primary labor markets

In such mobility experience, access to better labor markets comes at the cost of a mobility experience in which the journey to work requires more time and distance.

There are few alternatives by which workers in the mobility experience subtype VII can achieve an uncostly mobility situation. One of such strategies is to leave their places of residence in Eastern-MCMZ and to buy or rent a housing unit closer to employment subcenters. Such strategy produces the mobility experience presented in Figure 5.3 as subtype VIII, where the proximity between jobs and residence makes for a more pleasant commute. However, very few workers decide to relocate away from Eastern-MCMZ and closer to their formal jobs in the main employment subcenters. Participants of the study reported several explanations for the lack of relocation. One important reason has to do with higher land values in the zones closer to employment subcenters. Another reason has to do with the cost of living related to other consumer goods. Participants reported that consumer goods are more affordable in Eastern-MCMZ and become more expensive as they get closer to employment subcenters. Yet another reason has to do with social ties and support networks. Workers often do not relocate due to the fear of losing their social support networks. For example, the families of workers would usually support them with childcare while they go to work. Other participants mentioned that they would not leave Eastern-MCMZ because then there would be no one to take care of their elder family members.

Alternatively, some of the workers who have achieved access to better labor markets decide to become homeowners. Nevertheless, as land values near employment subcenters continue to outprice said workers from consumption, they often opt to go through the housing pathway provided by the national housing policy. Under this strategy, workers fall in the mobility experience depicted in Figure 5.3 as subtype IX, which operates like subtype IV and was presented in the previous section.

The production of default housing pathways

The results of the study highlight the emergence of default housing pathways that are producing a costly mobility experience for workers in Eastern-MCMZ. This default housing pathways are produced by the interplay between existing housing forms of production, the kinds of labor markets in which workers participate, and the institutional arrangements that determine which workers have access to which housing units. Such interplay is consistently pushing workers further into peripheral areas. Default housing pathways are steadily increasing the physical distance between workers and jobs, therefore increasing commuting costs for workers.

The workers without a formal job are tied to a default housing pathway based on the use value of housing. As explained earlier, workers without a formal job have no access to the housing stock produced through the national housing policy. As workers in the informal economy also tend to be low-income workers, they also lack access to housing loans through the private banking system. These restrictions leave them with no alternative but to look at whatever housing option is affordable and attainable, which often means buying a plot of land to build a housing unit by themselves. As land closer to employment subcenters is more expensive, affordable land is usually located in peripheral areas. After acquisition of their plot of land, informal workers engage in housing forms of production based on the use value of housing such as self-construction, construction by commission, or a combination of both.

The workers who do have a formal job are tied to a default housing pathway based on the national housing policy. Influential land and financial reform have paved the way for the preferred business model through which private developers participate in the current national housing policy. First, the pathbreaking land reform of 1992 allowed common agricultural land (known in Mexico as *ejidos*) to become private property and sold in the market. Second, the reforms of 1992, 1997, and 2000–2006 shaped the national housing policy as a bank-like system whose mission is to subsidize the production of housing units by private developers and to provide accessible credit for workers to buy a unit. Consequently, the preferred business model of private developers participating in the national housing policy has been to buy cheap agricultural land to produce affordable housing units at the lowest possible cost. Since the late 1990s and until today, most of the housing stock produced by the national housing policy is in peripheral areas toward the north and east of the MCMZ.

When workers with a formal job acquire a housing unit through the national housing policy, the default option is to get a housing unit in peripheral areas. This has severe implications for their mobility experience. Workers who are beneficiaries of the national housing policy and move to a housing unit in Eastern-MCMZ are tied to their formal jobs to continue to be beneficiaries of the program. Nevertheless, their formal jobs are usually within existing employment subcenters located in the center, west, or northwest of the MCMZ. This means that, by virtue of becoming homeowners and moving further into Eastern-MCMZ, their mobility experience becomes considerably costly overnight.

There are a couple of strategies that workers can resort to should they wish to escape these default housing pathways and improve their mobility experience. Both strategies consist of moving out of their housing unit in the periphery of Eastern-MCMZ but differ in their subsequent housing move. The first strategy consists of becoming home renters by looking for a rental housing unit closer to employment subcenters. The second consists of moving into some shared living arrangement by moving back with their parents or grandparents.

Conclusions

The mobility experience of workers is not only shaped by the location of jobs. In addition to the spatial location of the demand for labor, the mobility experience of workers is also influenced by the housing policies that influence their residential location. In some extreme cases, like in the case of Eastern-MCMZ, housing policies can sometimes produce default housing pathways that consistently increase the physical separation between jobs and workers. This chapter has provided a detailed explanation of the ways in which such default housing pathways are configured. As the chapter shows, the default housing pathways in which workers are caught can sometimes produce increases in transportation costs that shape inequalities in the mobility experience of workers. Most importantly, the chapter has shown that workers do not just choose to live in geographies of low accessibility. Instead, workers have no option but to live in such geographies due to the default housing pathways in which they are caught and the lack of housing alternatives.

Notes

1 For a textbook approach to mainstream location theory, see O'Sullivan (2018), Chapter 14, "The monocentric city and urban general equilibrium." For advanced discussion and critiques to location theory, see Park et al. (2020), Liu et al. (2021), and López-García and Baker (2022).

2 For a comprehensive review of the analytical elements in each housing form of production, see Jaramillo (1985) and Schteingart (1983, 1989).

3 For an overview of the main forms of housing production in MCMZ, see Schteingart (1989).

4 For a detailed account of Nezahualcoyotl's urbanization process, see Schteingart (1989), pp. 82–91.

References

Arenales, R., & Esquivel, M. T. (2012). El Bando 2: ¿Repoblamiento de la ciudad central? In E. Dahau (Ed.), *Ciudad de México: La construcción permanente de la metrópoli*. Quito: OLACCHI.

Barba, C., & Valencia, E. (2013). La transición del régimen de bienestar mexicano: Entre el dualismo y las reformas liberales. *Revista Uruguaya de Ciencia Política, 22*(2), 47–76.

Bettelheim, C. (1976). *Cálculo económico y formas de propiedad*. Ciudad de México: Siglo XXI.

Castillo, J. (2010). The promise of Neza: Building a city for 1.2 million inhabitants one house at the time. In I. Ruby & A. Ruby (Eds.), *Re-inventing construction*. Berlin: Ruby Press.

Clapham, D. (2002). Housing pathways: A post modern analytical framework. *Housing, Theory and Society, 19*(2), 57–68.

Clapham, D. (2003). Pathways approaches to homelessness research. *Journal of Community and Applied Social Psychology, 13*(2), 119–127.

Clapham, D. (2005). *The meaning of housing: A pathways approach*. Bristol: Policy Press.

Clapham, D., Mackie, P., Orford, S., Thomas, I., & Buckley, K. (2014). The housing pathways of young people in the UK. *Environment and Planning A, 46*(8), 2016–2031.

Cruz, F. (2015). *Configuración espacial de la industria en la Ciudad de México*. Ciudad de México: El Colegio de México.

Deng, W. J., Hoekstra, J., & Elsinga, M. (2020). The urban-rural discrepancy of generational housing pathways: A new source of intergenerational inequality in urban China? *Habitat International, 98*, 102102.

Flores, S., & Bornazou, E. (2012). El Bando 2: Balance de una política de reestructuración urbana. In A. Ziccardi (Ed.), *Ciudades del 2010: Entre la sociedad del conocimiento y la desigualdad social*. Ciudad de México: Universidad Nacional Autónoma de México.

García, B. (2010). Vivienda social en México (1940–1999). *Cuadernos de Vivenda y Urbanismo, 3*(5), 34–49.

Hamzah, H., & Zyed, Z. A. (2021). Housing pathways of young starters in urban Malaysia. *Journal of Housing and the Built Environment, 36*(2), 705–722.

Hiernaux, D., & Lindón, A. (2004). La periferia: Voz y sentido en los estudios urbanos. *Papeles de Población, 10*(42), 101–123.

Hochstenbach, C., & Boterman, W. R. (2015). Navigating the field of housing: Housing pathways of young people in Amsterdam. *Journal of Housing and the Built Environment, 30*(2), 257–274.

Jacquin, C. (2012). Producir y habitar la periferia. Los nuevos conjuntos de vivienda de bajo costo en México (ZMVM). *Bulletin de l'Institut Français d'études·Andines, 41*(3), 389–415.

Jaramillo, S. (1981). *Producción de vivienda y capitalismo dependiente. El caso de Bogotá*. Bogotá: CEDE.

Jaramillo, S. (1982). Las formas de producción del espacio construido en Bogotá. In E. Pradilla (Ed.), *Ensayos sobre el problema de la vivienda en América Latina*. Ciudad de México: UAM-Xochimilco.

Jaramillo, S. (1985). Las formas de producción de vivienda en Medellín 1930–1980. *Desarrollo y Sociedad, 17–18*, 53–102.

Jaramillo, S., & Schteingart, M. (1983). Procesos sociales y produccion de vivienda en América Latina: 1960–1980 (Analisis de casos). *Revista Mexicana de Sociología, 45*(1), 11–28.

Liu, D., Kwan, M. P., Kan, Z., & Song, Y. (2021). An integrated analysis of housing and transit affordability in the Chicago metropolitan area. *Geographical Journal, 187*(2), 110–126.

López-García, D., & Baker, D. (2022). Diverging mobility situations: Measuring relative job accessibility and differing socioeconomic conditions in New York City. *Annals of the Association of American Geographers*. Published online.

Monkkonen, P. (2011). The housing transition in Mexico: Expanding access to housing finance. *Urban Affairs Review, 47*(5), 672–695.

Negrete, M. E. (2000). Dinámica demográfica. In G. Garza (Ed.), *La Ciudad de México en el fin del segundo milenio*. Ciudad de México: El Colegio de México, Gobierno del Distrito Federal.

O'Sullivan, A. (2018). *Urban economics*. New York: McGraw-Hill Education.

Park, K., Ewing, R., Sabouri, S., Choi, D., Hamidi, S., & Tian, G. (2020). Guidelines for a polycentric region to reduce vehicle use and increase walking and transit use. *Journal of the American Planning Association, 86*(2), 236–249.

Quiroz, H. (2013). Elementos para una teoría de la ciudad mexicana contemporánea desde la práctica urbanística. *Andamios, Revista de Investigación Social, 10*(22), 113–128.

Rubalcava, R. M., & Schteingart, M. (2012). *Ciudades divididas: Desigualdad y segregación social en México*. Ciudad de México: El Colegio de México.

Schteingart, M. (1983). Producción de vivienda y sector inmobiliario (algunos elementos teóricos para su análisis). Revista Mexicana de Ciencias Políticas y Sociales, 28(111–2), 45–55.

Schteingart, M. (1989). *Los productores del espacio habitable: Estado, empresa y sociedad en la Ciudad de México*. Ciudad de México: El Colegio de México.

Wiesel, I. (2014). Mobilities of disadvantage: The housing pathways of low-income Australians. *Urban Studies, 51*(2), 319–334.

6 The spatial distribution of public and common mobility resources

This book argues that to really understand the underlying factors shaping inequalities in the mobility experience of workers, one must investigate the relationship between the availability of public transport systems and the spatial distribution of origins and destinations. Chapter 4 dealt with the distribution of destinations, where I presented a study about shifts in location of the demand for labor in MCMZ between 1999 and 2019. Chapter 5 dealt with the distribution of origins, where I presented a study of how housing policies are producing default housing pathways that push workers into the urban periphery and further away from employment subcenters. I will now deal with the availability of public transport systems in MCMZ.

This chapter takes a closer examination of the spatial distribution of *mobility resources* in MCMZ. For workers lacking a private vehicle, public transport systems are often the only mobility resource available to travel across urban space and reach the places offering urban jobs. The chapter complements the mobility resources literature with an analytical framework from the field of economics: the classification of goods and services by their level of excludability and rivalry of consumption. In doing so, I develop a methodology to explore the public and private nature of mobility resources and classify them into four categories: private, club, public, and common mobility resources. Specifically, the chapter maps the spatial distribution of *public* and *common* mobility resources, as their provision almost always relies on the public sector. The study of publicly funded mobility resources shows the existing spatial inequalities in how the public transport systems connects workers from their origins to their destinations. Finally, the chapter builds on semi-structured interviews with key informants to explore why public and common mobility resources tend to be located in proximity to employment subcenters and further away from Eastern-MCMZ.

Analytical strategy and research methods

Mobility resources are defined as infrastructure or systems that enable or facilitate peoples' travel across cities in some way (Kowald et al., 2017; Le Vine et al., 2013; Loder & Axhausen, 2018). Scholars in the field of mobility resources have traditionally centered their attention on studying resources that are owned by individuals: the privately owned mobility resources (Habib et al., 2018;

DOI: 10.4324/9781003261698-6

Kowald et al., 2017; Le Vine et al., 2013; Loder & Axhausen, 2018; Plevka et al., 2018). However, there is increasing recognition that the mixed private and public nature of mobility resources has not been prominently addressed by the literature (Loder & Axhausen, 2018).

Aiming to narrow this gap, this chapter follows the steps of scholars like Frischmann (2012) and Ho (2019) and introduces nuances to the mobility resources literature by resorting to an analytical framework from the field of economics: the classification of goods and services by their level of excludability and rivalry of consumption. A good is *nonrival* when "a unit of the good can be consumed by one individual without detracting, in the slightest, from the consumption opportunities still available to others from that same unit" (Cornes & Sandler, 1996, p. 8). A good is excludable when the benefits of providing that good can be withheld through a price mechanism, and non-excludable when the benefits provided by the good are available to all regardless of the price (Cornes & Sandler, 1996, p. 8). According to mainstream microeconomics (Cornes & Sandler, 1996), goods and services can be classified into four categories according to their level of excludability and rivalry of consumption: private goods, public goods, toll (club) goods, and common goods.

This analytical framework can be used to unpack mobility resources and classify them into four categories according to their level of excludability and rivalry of consumption (Figure 6.1). First, *private mobility resources* are those privately owned for which people must pay (excludable) and their use is limited to the person paying (rival). Examples of private mobility resources include a private car, petrol, a private bicycle, or a motorcycle. Second, *public mobility resources* are those to which people have free access (non-excludable), and every person can use them regardless of how other people use them (nonrival). Examples of public mobility resources are the free shuttle buses assuming enough seats, the Staten Island Ferry in New York City, sidewalks, or streets for cars. Third, *common mobility resources* are those that every person can use for free (non-excludable) but could become scarce and even depleted if many people use them (rival). Examples include a free bicycle sharing system or a free public transit system provided by the city assuming that there are not enough seats. Fourth, *club mobility resources* are those that will not become scarce if many

Private Mobility resources	**Public mobility resources**	**Toll (club) mobility resources**	**Common mobility resources**
Excludable and Rival	*Nonexcludable and nonrival*	*Excludable but nonrival*	*Rival but nonexcludable*
- Personal car - Petrol - Driving license - Personal bicycle - Personal motorcycle - Passport	- Sidewalks - Disability ramps - Free public transit systems - Streetlights	- Parking Spaces (if there is a toll) - Private bike sharing program - Concessioned transit systems	- Parking Spaces (if free) - Public bike sharing program - Public transit systems - Streets and avenues

Figure 6.1 Classification of some mobility resources according to the level of excludability and rivalry of consumption

people use them (nonrival), but people must pay to access them (excludable). Examples include concessioned bus systems assuming there are enough seats, or car-sharing programs.

The classification presented in Figure 6.1 is not clear-cut and, once classified, mobility resources do not remain static within a category. Mobility resources can shift across categories according to fluctuations in two characteristics: (i) the level of congestion, and (ii) price relative to income. The consumption of common and club goods involves sharing, which often leads to a partial rivalry of benefits as larger memberships crowd one another. Congestion occurs when one user's consumption of the good decreases the benefits or the quality of service still available to the remaining users (Cornes & Sandler, 1996, p. 348). When applied to the classification of mobility resources, congestion means that the mobility resources that are in principle non-rival can become rival as congestion increases. A classic example would be an avenue that remains empty during traffic's non-peak hours but becomes unbearably congested during peak hours. As conveyed by this hypothetical example, as congestion increases, a mobility resource that could be classified as a public good can become instead a common good.

There is also the price characteristic. According to Cornes and Sandler (1996, p. 349), the price is an exclusion mechanism through which nonmembers and/or nonpayers can be barred from consumption. Nevertheless, to assess whether a price will achieve its goal of excluding users from using mobility resources, it is essential to consider price elasticity of demand. Price elasticity of demand measures the responsiveness in the quantity demanded of a good or service, relative to changes in the price of that good or service (Steinemann, Apgar & Brown, 2005, p. 35). Several factors influence price elasticity of demand, one of which is expenditures relative to income: "the larger the percentage of a consumer's income that is spent for a good, the more price elastic the demand for that good can be" (Steinemann et al., 2005, p. 36). It follows that when the price to use a mobility resource takes a larger share of the user's income, that user's demand will be more elastic. This means that decreases in the price of mobility resources will have a larger effect on the low-income population than in the middle- or high-income population.

Mapping public mobility resources

The data used for the mapping of public mobility resources in the MCMZ are taken from the National Housing Inventory (INV-2016) developed in 2016 by the National Institute of Statistics, Geography and Informatics (INEGI, by its acronym in Spanish). The INV-2016 allows access to data at the block level for the following indicators: paved streets, availability of sidewalks, availability of ramps for wheelchairs, availability of streetlights, and displays of street names. These are useful indicators to assess public mobility resources because these kinds of urban infrastructures facilitate people's travel across the city and are both non-rival and non-excludable. After careful consideration of the five available indicators, the decision was made to use only three: paved streets, availability of sidewalks, and availability of streetlights. The indicators of availability of ramps for wheelchairs and displays of street names were discarded due to their possible ambiguity.[1] The values for the indicators are ordinal and measured in the following ways: all streets, some of the streets, none of the streets, non-specified, and *housing complex*.

Once the indicators were selected, a compound index of public mobility resources was calculated. The first step was to normalize the selected indicators by rescaling their values taking them to the range [0,1] (Schuschny & Soto, 2009). An analysis at the block level was conducted to assign values to the ordinal categories in the following scale: all streets = 1, some of the streets = 0.5, none of the streets = 0, housing complex = 1. The categories "non-specified" were taken out of the analysis. Once values at the block level were assigned, the average for the blocks comprising each census tract was calculated. After obtaining the average for each indicator at the census tract level, a compound indicator was calculated by averaging the values of the three selected indicators. This technique produced a value at the census tract level for the compound indicator *public mobility resources* within the range [0,1]. As the value of the indicator gets closer to 1, the census tract is provisioned with more public mobility resources. As the value of the indicator gets closer to 0, the census tract has less public mobility resources. Finally, the compound indicator was analyzed using geographical information systems (GIS) and five categories were created using natural breaks: low (0 to 0.36), medium-low (0.37 to 0.58), medium (0.59 to 0.74), medium-high (0.75 to 0.89), and high (0.90 to 1).

Mapping common mobility resources

As discussed in the previous section, policies that lower the fare of mass transport systems can transform a mobility resource that is potentially excludable into one that is non-excludable. Under this logic, the common mobility resources being mapped in this study are the mass transport infrastructures that are state-owned or those whose operation and fare are highly subsidized by the state. Specifically, in the case of Mexico City, I consider the subway system (*Sistema de Transporte Colectivo Metro*), two publicly owned bus companies (*Servicios de Transportes Eléctricos* [STE] and *Red de Transporte de Pasajeros* [RTP]), and the Bus Rapid Transit system (Metrobús). In the case of the State of Mexico, I consider the Bus Rapid Transit system (Mexibús) and the Suburban Railroad system (*Tren Suburbano*). The municipality of Tizayuca, in the State of Hidalgo, has no mass transit infrastructure that could be classified as a common mobility resource.

The data for the calculation of the common mobility resources were taken from two sources. First, the data for Mexico City were accessed through the Mexico City Open Data webpage, which provides georeferenced files locating the stations, stops, and terminals of what the city calls the unified mass transit system and includes the selected mass transit infrastructures. Second, the data for the State of Mexico were accessed through the DOT MX project webpage,[2] which provides georeferenced files locating the stations of the State of Mexico's Bus Rapid Transit system (Mexibús) and the Suburban Railroad system.

Once data were collected, I proceeded to calculate an *access index* for the common mobility resources available in the MCMZ. An access index measures the availability of common mobility resources at the census tract level by identifying the service area of the selected mass transit infrastructures (Bhat et al., 2005, p. 12). The calculation of the access index was made with geographic information systems (GIS) through a series of steps. The stations, stops, and terminals of the selected mass transit systems were mapped, and a 500-meter buffer from each of them was drawn. The 500-meter buffer is a criterion commonly used in the field of mass transit accessibility (Bhat et al., 2005, p. 12). Then, an analysis was conducted to count how many buffers intersect with the centroid of each census tract. A table with the number of times each centroid intersects with a buffer was made. According to this table, the census tract with the most access to common mobility resources is touched by 42 buffers, while 62 percent of the census tract centroids in MCMZ are not touched by any buffer.

The next step was to calculate a normalized access index. The normalization process consisted of rescaling the number of times a census tract centroid intersects with a buffer to a scale in the range [1,0]. To do so, I employed the distance between the maximum and the minimum values in the table (Schuschny & Soto, 2009, p. 58). The maximum value was 42 and the minimum value was 0. As the value of the index approaches 1, the census tract has more access to common mobility resources. As the value of the index approaches 0, the census tract has less access to common mobility resources. Finally, the compound indicator was analyzed using geographical information systems (GIS). Five categories were created using a natural breaks analysis: low (0.02 to 0.12), medium-low (0.13 to 0.26), medium (0.27 to 0.43), medium-high (0.44 to 0.62), and high (0.63 to 1).

Research results

The MCMZ spreads across 220,752.8 Ha, and 46.5 percent of its territory has a high or medium-high provision of public mobility resources, while only 4.6 percent of the territory has low provision (Table 6.1). The provision of public mobility resources in the MCMZ shows a concentric spatial pattern, with increased provision in the central area of the metropolitan region and lower delivery in peripheral areas (Map 6.1). The Map 6.1 shows the spatial distribution of public mobility resources across the metropolitan region. As the map shows, most of Mexico City's territory falls within the categories of high and medium-high. The areas with a majority of a medium-low and low provision of public mobility resources are the peripheral zones in the south of Mexico City. In the case of the State of Mexico, Map 6.1 shows that the only zones that can be regarded as having a good provision of public mobility resources are in the west of the MCMZ.

Table 6.1 Distribution of public and common mobility resources in the MCMZ (Ha)

	No MR	*Low*	*Medium low*	*Medium*	*Medium high*	*High*
Public mobility resources (PMR)		10,081.6 (4.6%)	54,129.7 (24.5%)	53,948.8 (24.4%)	52,000.9 (23.6%)	50,591.7 (22.9%)
Common mobility resources (CMR)	155,079.1 (70.3%)	34,841 (15.8%)	18,011.6 (8.2%)	8,976.9 (4.1%)	2,887.1 (1.3%)	956.7 (0.4%)

	Above the mean in both categories	*Above the mean only in PMR*	*Above the mean only in CMR*	*Below the mean in both categories*
Above or below the MCMZ mean	17,891.2 (8.1%)	76,937.1 (34.9%)	1,560.9 (0.7%)	124,363.6 (56.3%)

Source: Author's calculations with data from the 2016 National Housing Inventory, the Open Data webpage of the Mexico City Government, and the DOT MX project

The provision of common mobility resources in MCMZ can be described as highly unequal. Table 6.1 shows that 70.3 percent of the metropolitan region's territory lack any kind of common mobility resource while only 1.7 percent of the territory has high or medium-high provision. Map 6.2 shows the spatial distribution of common mobility resources across the MCMZ. The map shows that most common mobility resources are located within Mexico City, specifically along two corridors that spread along the central municipalities. Map 6.2 also shows that the vast majority of the State of Mexico's territory lacks common mobility resources. The only census tracts in the State of Mexico with common mobility resources are within the category "low." These census tracts are located along mass transit infrastructures such as the subway lines A and B, the three routes of the Mexibús Bus Rapid Transit system, and the Suburban Railroad system.

Finally, the extent to which the MCMZ provides salient levels of both public and common mobility resources to its inhabitants was analyzed. To do so, the census tracts were classified into four categories. The first category shows the census tracts that are above the metropolitan average in both public and common mobility resources. The second category shows the census tracts above the mean only in the public mobility resources indicator, but below the mean in common mobility resources. The third category shows the census tracts above the average in common mobility resources, but below the mean in public mobility resources. Lastly, the fourth category shows the census tracts that are below the mean in both public and common mobility resources. Table 6.1 shows that only 8.1 percent of the city's territory is above the mean in both categories of mobility resources, while 56.3 percent is below both means.

Map 6.3 shows the spatial distribution of the census tracts that are above the mean in both categories of mobility resources. The Map 6.3 also identifies the boundaries of existing employment subcenters in 2019 as presented in

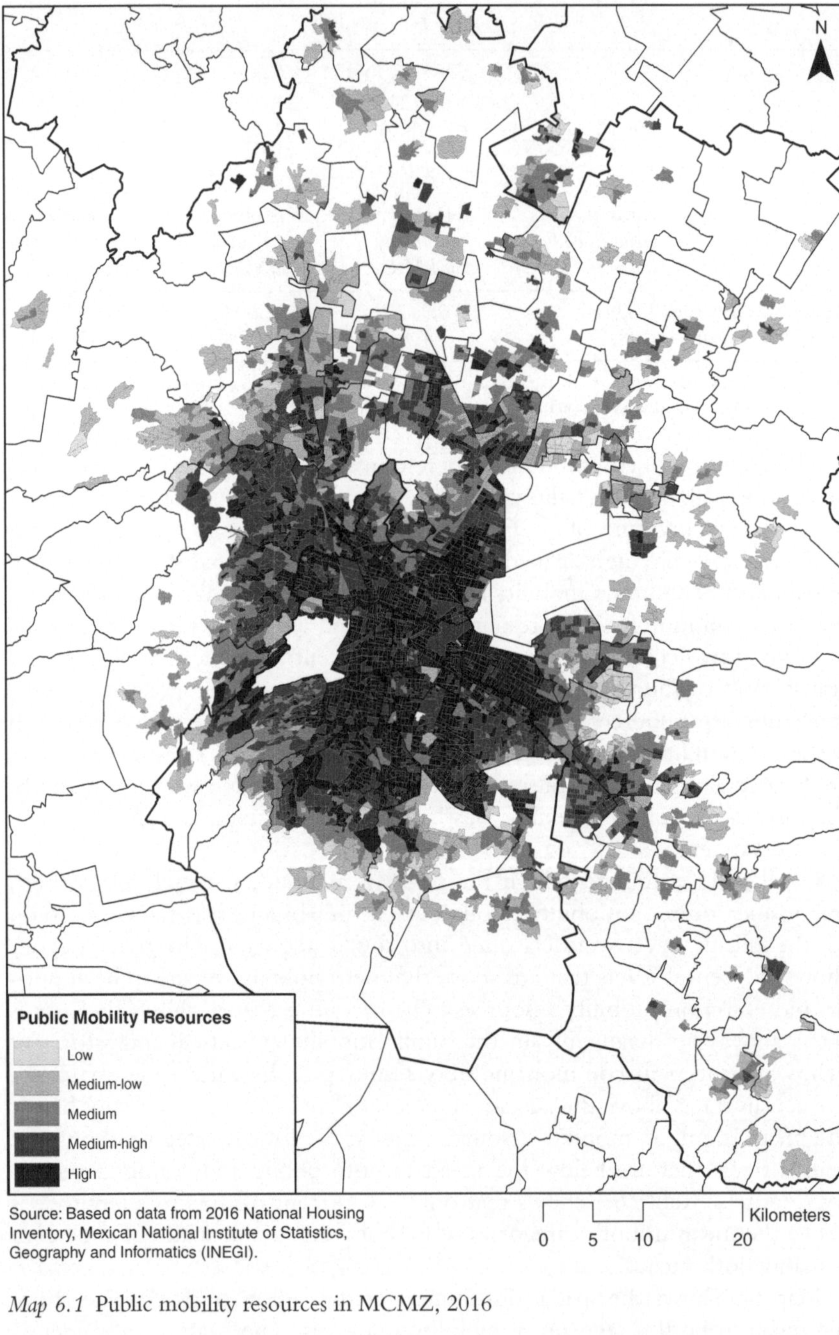

Map 6.1 Public mobility resources in MCMZ, 2016

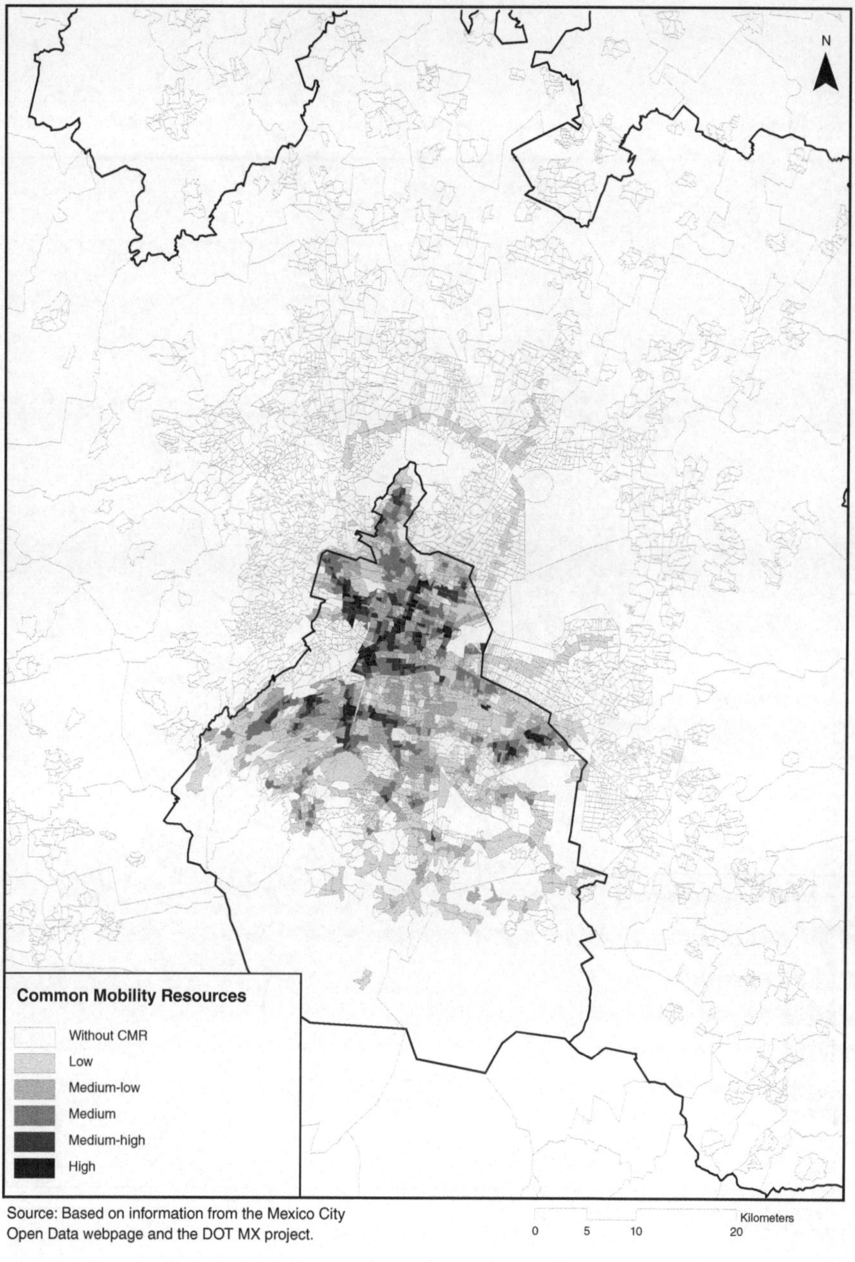

Map 6.2 Common mobility resources in MCMZ, 2020

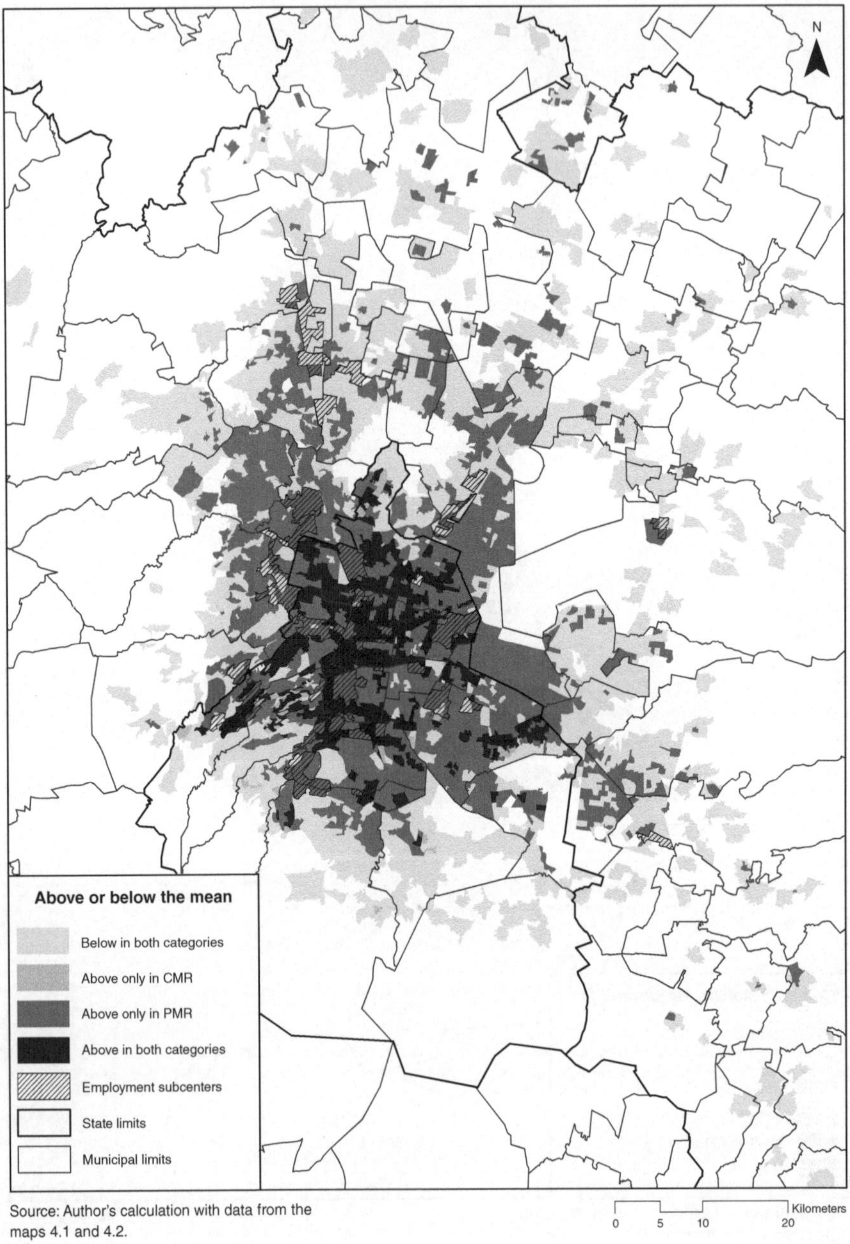

Map 6.3 Joint public and common mobility resources in MCMZ

Chapter 4. Several characteristics can be highlighted. First, most of the territory above the mean in both categories of mobility resources overlaps with or is in the proximity of existing employment subcenters. Second, Eastern-MCMZ falls behind in the provision of common mobility resources and most of its territory is below the mean in both categories of mobility resources.

The political economy of public and common mobility resources

The semi-structured interviews allowed to identify some aspects of the political economy of transport that have operated to pull investment in public and common mobility resources toward existing employment subcenters, and away from Eastern-MCMZ.[3] First, the intense process of urbanization in Eastern-MCMZ[4] brought a large increase in the population's transport needs. The local and state governments have been unable to provide public transport as a public good within the newly urbanized territories. Given the absence of the state in providing public transport as a public good, the population of Eastern-MCMZ has had no option but to satisfy their transportation requirements by using the services of private providers of public transport. The increasing transport needs of the population, then, was constituted into a new source of wealth in and of itself. This new source of urban wealth was left to be captured. The vacuum left by the absence of the state has been occupied by private actors that, both formally and informally, have organized to provide the transport services needed by the population.

Second, there is a general perception among interviewees that public transit in Eastern-MCMZ is ungovernable and that local authorities lack the capacity to implement the policies that they plan. However, this generalized perception was complemented by interviewees with an explanation about the local authorities' incapacity to govern public transit: the emergence of the private providers of public transport and their organizations as powerful political actors in their own right. Known as *transportistas*, these groups have achieved considerable influence in the transport policy subsystem and important veto power. According to the interviewees, the *transportistas* have achieved such political power by assembling both an electoral machine and a system of material incentives. Over the years, politicians running for local government and the leadership of the *transportistas* have reached an agreement of public transport concessions in exchange for votes. The number of people behind each organization of the *transportistas* could reach several hundreds, or even thousands.[5] In exchange for the organization's votes, politicians would agree to lobby for more concessioned bus routes and to protect the *transportistas* territory by not allowing the entry of more public transport providers. Once in office, according to the interviewees, politicians would receive a small share of the *transportistas*' profits as an arrangement that would keep the partnership in place. This system of material incentives is only possible due to the commodification of the population's transport needs. As such, the preferred transport policy solution by the

State of Mexico's local government has historically been a concessions system in which public transport is privately owned and managed.

A third explanation for the lack of public and common mobility resources in Eastern-MCMZ has to do with the prevailing transit planning paradigm at place in MCMZ. When discussing the government's planning approach to transport, interviewees explained how this approach is usually based on providing transport solutions to preexisting transportation demands. Interviewees explained how in Eastern-MCMZ the population ended up in the residential locations that they could get their hands on, and the government arrived years later to try to solve their transportation problems. The transit planning paradigm in MCMZ is one of reactions to preexisting mobility needs, as opposed to practicing future-scenario planning.

Under this transit planning paradigm, interviewees highlighted that the territories that lack a public transit policy are usually served by an array of informal transport infrastructures. Systems such as informal buses, informal taxis, bicitaxis (bicycle taxis), and mototaxis (motorcycle taxis) have emerged to provide last-mile transit solutions and even as the main transit infrastructure in many peripheral neighborhoods. There are mixed perceptions among participants of this study about the merits of informal transport systems. Some interviewees highlight that these informal transport systems operate like transport cartels that profit from workers' mobility needs. These informal transport networks often constitute themselves as important political actors with veto power, thus becoming an important player in the policy subsystem of transport solutions. Other interviewees highlighted the positive aspects of informal transport systems, such as being an affordable option, extending the hours of transport service, or even their role in providing safe mobility options for women who often trust the regular drivers.

The lack of public transport as a public and common good in Eastern-MCMZ is also explained by the high political fragmentation of the metropolitan region. The MCMZ is a tri-state area comprising 76 mayoralties and municipalities. Except for rare circumstances, Mexico City has had one type of transport system and the State of Mexico has had a different one. Each system would provide service only within their political demarcation and will not do so beyond its political boundaries. This political fragmentation is problematic because it has hampered the possibility of pursuing a public transport policy at a metropolitan scale. There were times when coordination between authorities in Mexico City and the State of Mexico was more feasible. This was especially true between the late 1980s and the mid-1990s, when the subway system was extended beyond the political boundaries of Mexico City and into the State of Mexico through Lines A and B. This was also the time when new institutional spaces for metropolitan public transport policy were created, such as the Metropolitan Commission for Transport and Roads (COMETRAVI, by its acronym in Spanish). This momentum for metropolitan coordination, however, seems to have been the outcome of political alignment between the government of Mexico City, the State of Mexico, and the Federal Government, as the three of them belonged to the same political party, the Institutional Revolution Party (PRI, by its acronym in Spanish). This political alignment ended in 1998 when the left-wing Democratic Revolution Party (PRD, by its acronym in Spanish) won Mexico City's government. Since then, metropolitan coordination in transport policy has been a difficult goal to achieve. Today, political actors and appointed officials in transport agencies acknowledge the constraints imposed by political fragmentation.

This political divide between Mexico City and the State of Mexico is problematic because the provision of public transport as a public and common good in both political demarcations has followed very different paths. In the case of Mexico City, there is a long-standing tradition of providing public transport as a public and common good. In Mexico City, the preferred transport policy has been a mix between a concessions system and state-owned transport companies. Through this mix, Mexico City has traditionally subsidized the cost of urban transport through infrastructure such as the subway system built in the late 1960s, and the state-owned bus company Ruta-100 constituted in 1981. When Ruta-100 declared bankruptcy in 1995, the city retained a portion of the state-owned bus company that is still publicly owned and managed today under the name of Passenger Transport Network (RTP, by its acronym in Spanish). The newest transport innovation in Mexico City, the Bus Rapid Transit (BRT) Metrobús, a public–private partnership, retains this principle as the city government heavily subsidizes the operation of the BRT to keep the fare as low as possible.

In the case of the State of Mexico, the preferred transport policy has by and large been the provision of public transport through a concessions system. Except for a short-lived state-owned bus company called *Sistema de Transporte Troncal* (Corridor Transport Systems) between 1982 and 1992, the State of Mexico has not engaged in any kind of direct subsidy in transportation policy. In the State of Mexico, concessioned bus systems and informal transport services are the norm. The latest transit system improvement in Eastern-MCMZ is the BRT Mexibús. This system is operated through a public–private partnership in which the government of the State of Mexico provides the infrastructure and subsidizes the system's operation to guarantee the private bus providers revenue. While Mexibús represents a step in the right direction, it is still a very modest one compared with the transportation needs of Eastern-MCMZ.

Finally, a force pulling investment in public and common mobility resources toward the Central Agglomeration has to do with trendy urbanism and the goals of sustainable and efficient transport systems. As the account of interviewees suggested, trendy urbanism (Whitney, 2021) related to sustainable urbanization works in favor of capital. Under the argument of stopping unsustainable urban sprawl, many well-intentioned advocacy groups such as the World Resources Institute (WRI) or the Institute for Transportation and Development Policy (ITDP), among others, have inadvertently supported the nested agenda of capital. A good example of this kind of politics is the process to decide the location of the first Mexico City BRT line in 2004. Two options were on the table. The first one was Eje-8 Ermita, a main avenue in Iztapalapa in Eastern-MCMZ. The second option was Insurgentes Avenue, which runs through the heart of the Central

Agglomeration. The decision was made to locate the BRT in the latter location, at the heart of the main employment subcenter of the metropolitan region.

As explained by interviewees, the decision about the location of the first BRT line was made based on sustainable urbanization and efficiency arguments. First and foremost, policymakers believed that locating the first BRT line of Mexico City at the heart of its main economic agglomeration would send a powerful political message that the city government was fully committed with sustainable transit. This, in turn, was believed to help in the policy process to advance the transformation of old and polluting buses across the city into modern, low-emission, and efficient BRT systems. Second, the decision was heavily influenced by neoclassical economic thinking and its policy decision frameworks based on principles of efficiency. When members of the policy subsystem argued about which location would yield the greatest impact, the conversation was framed within techniques to quantify utility and using marginal analysis as a rule of thumb for decision making. By any measure, the available decision-making frameworks such as cost-benefit analysis indicated that locating the BRT line in the Central Agglomeration would maximize the benefits of the infrastructure's investment. When framed in that way, locating the BRT in Insurgentes Avenue was seen as the right policy choice. Sixteen years have passed and Eje-8 Ermita, in Eastern-MCMZ, continues without a BRT line or any upcoming plan to build one.

Conclusions

This chapter studied the spatial distribution of publicly funded *mobility resources* in MCMZ. A theoretical framework was developed that allowed the study of the public and private nature of mobility resources. By conceptualizing and mapping what in this chapter is called *public* and *common* mobility resources, the chapter shows the spatial distribution of mobility resources in the MCMZ. Overall, the chapter brings empirical evidence to support the hypothesis that the MCMZ has pursued an inequitable course of infrastructure investment into existing employment subcenters to the detriment of the peripheral areas. The spatial distribution of public and common mobility resources in the MCMZ is worryingly unequal. Virtually, the totality of the common mobility resources is localized in Mexico City, leaving the State of Mexico lagging in its provision. Mexico City has a long-standing tradition of providing common mobility resources to its inhabitants. In contrast, the State of Mexico provides disturbingly low levels of common mobility resources—in many places, none.

Several factors of the political economy of transport have contributed to produce the unequal transport geography depicted by this chapter. When the state fails to provide public transport as a public and common good, urbanization creates a new kind of wealth embodied in the population's transportation needs. In the absence of the state, the wealth is there for the grab of private providers of public transport. Over time, private providers of public transport have constituted themselves as powerful political actors in their own right, with important veto power, and have become important players in the policy subsystem of public transport. Private providers of public transport take advantage of the high levels of political fragmentation in the MCMZ and different transport policies across political demarcations. While Mexico City has maintained a tradition of providing public transport as a public and common good since at least the late 1960s, the State of Mexico has maintained a tradition of commodifying public transport. Finally, investment in public transport as public and common mobility resources has been further pulled into the central economic agglomeration by framing the discussion about transport policy in terms of sustainable urbanization and economic efficiency principles.

Notes

1 Ambiguity in the "ramps for wheelchairs" and "display of street names" indicators comes from the value given to the indicator as "housing complex." When a block is classified as a *housing complex*, it is safe to assume that the complex has at least paved streets, sidewalks, and streetlights. Nevertheless, the assumption that the housing complex has ramps for wheelchairs and displays for street names cannot be made with the same confidence.

2 Proyecto DOT MX: http://itdp.mx/dotmx

3 As described in the introductory chapter of the book, the investigation of the political economy behind the spatial distribution of public and common mobility resources in MCMZ is based on semi-structured interviews with 34 key informants coming from urban development and mobility experts, government officials, civil society organizations, and academia.

4 As it was explained in depth in Chapter 5, Eastern-MCMZ has been consistently urbanizing since the 1950s in several waves and through different mechanisms. First, rural migrant workers in the 1950s and 1960s who were determined to acquire a piece of land in Nezahualcóyotl for self-construction (Schteingart, 1989). Then, the second and third generations of Nezahualcóyotl settlers unfolding into Chimalhuacán and La Paz since the 1970s. A third wave started in the 1980s, when social movements such as *Movimiento Antorchista* mobilized the urban poor into the social production of habitat in places like Chimalhuacán, Chicoloapan, and Ixtapaluca (Lina & Rodríguez, 2003). A fourth and most recent wave started in the 1990s, when the national housing policy produced thousands of new social housing developments for the working class in Ixtapaluca, Chicoloapan, and Chalco (Jacquin, 2012).

5 According to an interviewee with inside knowledge of the *transportistas* organization, a union of *transportistas* is usually composed of several routes. Each route has a leader and several delegates per shift. Each delegate is responsible for several route supervisors (*checadores*) who control the bus traffic on the ground. In addition, there are the bus owners, one to two bus drivers per bus, and a person per shift in each bus trying to get as much ridership as possible in each unit.

References

Bhat, C. R., Guo, J. Y., Sen, S., & Weston, L. (2005). *Measuring access to public transportation services: Review of customer-oriented transit performance measures and methods of transit submarket identification*. Austin, TX: Center for Transportation Research, The University of Texas at Austin.

Cornes, R., & Sandler, T. (1996). *The theory of externalities, public goods and club goods* (2nd ed.). Cambridge: Cambridge University Press.

Frischmann, B. M. (2012). *Infrastructure: The social value of shared resources*. Oxford: Oxford University Press.

Habib, K. N., Weiss, A., & Hasnine, S. (2018). On the heterogeneity and substitution patterns in mobility tool ownership choices of post-secondary students: The case of Toronto. *Transportation Research Part A: Policy and Practice*, *116*, 650–665.

Ho, S. (2019). *Thirsty cities: Social contracts and public goods provision in China and India*. Cambridge: Cambridge University Press.

Jacquin, C. (2012). Producir y habitar la periferia. Los nuevos conjuntos de vivienda de bajo costo en México (ZMVM). *Bulletin de l'Institut Français d'études Andines*, *41*(3), 389–415.

Kowald, M., Kieser, B., Mathys, N., & Justen, A. (2017). Determinants of mobility resource ownership in Switzerland: Changes between 2000 and 2010. *Transportation*, *44*(5), 1–23.

Le Vine, S., Lee-Gosselin, M., Sivakumar, A., & Polak, J. (2013). A new concept of accessibility to personal activities: Development of theory and application to an empirical study of mobility resource holdings. *Journal of Transport Geography*, *31*, 1–10.

Lina, P., & Rodríguez, H. (2003). El espacio social de la ciudad de Ixtapaluca: Proceso de periurbanización de la Ciudad de México. *Scripta Nova: Revista Electrónica de Geografía y Ciencias Sociales*, *VII*, *146*(042).

Loder, A., & Axhausen, K. W. (2018). Mobility tools and use: Accessibility's role in Switzerland. *The Journal of Transport and Land Use*, *11*(1), 367–385.

Plevka, V., Astegiano, P., Himpe, W., Tampère, C., & Vandebroek, M. (2018). How personal accessibility and frequency of travel affect ownership decisions on mobility resources. *Sustainability (Switzerland)*, *10*(4), 1–25.

Schteingart, M. (1989). *Los productores del espacio habitable: Estado, empresa y sociedad en la Ciudad de México*. Ciudad de México: El Colegio de México.

Schuschny, A., & Soto, H. (2009). *Guía metodológica: Diseño de indicadores compuestos de desarrollo sostenible*. Documento de Proyecto. Santiago de Chile: Comisión Económica para América Latina y el Caribe (CEPAL).

Steinemann, A. C., Apgar, W. C., & Brown, H. J. (2005). *Microeconomics for public decisions*. Mason: Thomson, South-Western.

Whitney, R. (2021). Trendy urbanists, innovation laboratories, and best practices: In pursuit of "progressive" urban planning in Mexico City. *Town Planning Review*, *93*(1), 15–35.

7 Conclusion

Policy interactions and the choiceless mobility hypothesis

The purpose of this book is to investigate the policy interactions that have shaped inequalities in the mobility experience of workers in MCMZ. To do so, several empirical studies have been presented throughout the book. In Chapter 3, I presented a study of time and distance in the journey to work in MCMZ to map the spatial distribution of mobility situations across MCMZ. I then argued that to really understand the underlying factors that shape inequalities in the mobility experience of workers, one must look at the relationship between the availability of transport systems and the spatial distributions and sorting of origins and destinations. Aiming to look at that relationship, Chapter 4 presented a study about the shift in the spatial location of the demand for labor in MCMZ between 1999 and 2019. Then, Chapter 5 investigated the origins of trips through a study about how housing policies produce default housing pathways in MCMZ that are pushing workers further into peripheral areas. Finally, Chapter 6 looked at the availability of transport systems by looking at the spatial distributions of public and common mobility resources across the MCMZ.

The purpose of this chapter is to apply the Policy Interactions Framework (PIF) to the findings from the empirical studies presented in Chapters 3, 4, 5, and 6. The PIF is designed as analytical lens for the empirical study of how policies from distinct policy domains overlap in urban space and interact to produce specific urban outcomes.[1] Two specific policy interactions were identified and are explained in detail. As an outcome of applying the PIF, the chapter develops and puts forward the choiceless mobility hypothesis (CMH), defined as the process through which the interaction between policies from distinct policy domains produce mobility situations that consistently increase the transportation costs for workers. The chapter provides a detailed discussion of how the CMH is different from other concepts available in the transport and accessibility literature and ends with a discussion about the implications of the CMH for urban policy analysis.

Identifying policy interactions

Applying the PIF to the studies presented in the previous chapters allowed the identification of two specific policy interactions. The first is an interaction between the intense urbanization of Eastern-MCMZ and the emergence

DOI: 10.4324/9781003261698-7

of local private providers of public transport as powerful political actors. The second is an interaction between economic development and housing policies that is constantly increasing the commuting costs for workers. In what follows, I describe both policy interactions in detail.

Urbanization and the emergence of **transportistas** *as powerful political actors*

The first policy interaction identified by this study is depicted in Figure 7.1. As explained in previous chapters, Eastern-MCMZ urbanized rapidly due to the national imports substitution policy and industrialization of Mexico City during the 1940s–1960s (see Chapter 5). The prohibition of *Regente* Uruchurtu in 1964 to build new housing units within Mexico City's political boundaries left no option for migrant workers and low-income population than to look for shelter in the neighboring State of Mexico. Nevertheless, employment subcenters continued to cluster toward the center, west, and northwest of the MCMZ (see Chapter 4). The ever-growing physical separation between employment subcenters and workers' location consistently increased the mobility needs of residents in Eastern-MCMZ (see Chapter 3). In the absence of the state to provide public transport as a public or common mobility resource (see Chapter 6), such mobility needs have produced a new source of urban wealth because workers must pay to satisfy their mobility needs. There was a brief period between 1982 and 1992 in which the government of the State of Mexico provided public transport service through the state-owned *Sistema de Transporte Troncal* (Corridor Transport Systems)—a system that contributed to de-commodify public transport in the region. Nevertheless, the corridor transport system was dismantled in 1992 and substituted by a concessions system.

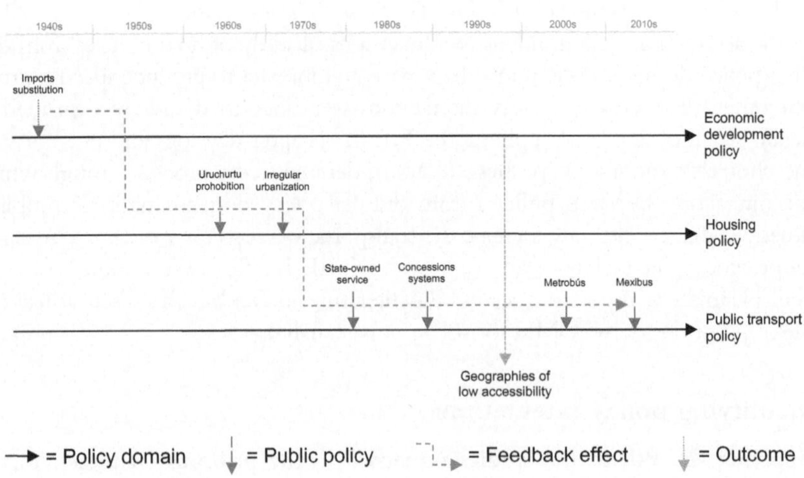

Figure 7.1 Policy interaction I

This new source of urban wealth was left for the grab of whoever mobilized to capture it. Since then, the mobility needs of workers in Eastern-MCMZ have been traditionally satisfied by private providers of public transport and their organizations called *transportistas* (transporters).

Over time, the *transportistas* have constituted themselves as powerful political organizations and have attained important influence over public transport policy. Here lies some of the feedback effects between policy domains that are at the heart of the policy interaction shown in Figure 7.1. Economic development and housing policies originated *resources effects* that looped back into public transport policy. Because private providers of public transport were there to meet the transportation needs of workers, the intense urbanization of Eastern-MCMZ distributed resources among the *transportistas*. These resources have created incentives for the *transportistas* to mobilize politically and advocate to expand their service coverage. This, in turn, has produced ever-increasing resources for their organizations thus strengthening their position to advocate for their interests.

There have also been important *interpretive effects*. After decades operating in Eastern-MCMZ, the role of *transportistas* as a legitimate policy solution to the problem of the workers' transportation needs has been accepted and stabilized among social and governmental actors. The transition toward the concessions system in the early 1990s contributed to a growing consensus that the private sector was better equipped than the state to deal with the transportation needs of workers in peripheral MCMZ. Furthermore, the interpretive effects have produced a shared understanding among relevant actors that *transportistas* have a legitimate say in the policy process around public transport policy. With somewhat of a monopoly over the flow of workers in Eastern-MCMZ and the thread of a transportation strike, the *transportistas* have achieved important veto power over policy alternatives.

The interpretive effects around *transportistas* looped back to public transport policy in many ways, but its effects on the policy process for the implementation of Bus Rapid Transit (BRT) systems in MCMZ is a case in point. The introduction in 2005 of the Metrobús system in Mexico City paved the way for BRT adoption by the neighboring State of Mexico, who in 2010 introduced the Mexibús system. The Mexibús line that runs through Eastern-MCMZ—the Line 3 that runs from Pantitlán in Mexico City proper to Chimalhuacán in the State of Mexico—started operations in 2013. In both BRT systems, governments had to negotiate with the *transportista*s organizations that controlled the minibus routes overlapping with the BRT system routes. Implementing agencies and *transportistas* agreed to establish a public–private partnership (PPP). Through this PPP, the *transportistas* bus-owners and drivers would be included in the operation of the BRT system, who would still be operating by a for-profit logic. Without these kinds of compromises, the *transportistas* would have been able to use their veto power to stop BRT implementation. Today, transport policies in Eastern-MCMZ must be carefully negotiated with the *transportistas*.

Economic development and housing policies are increasing commuting costs

The second policy interaction identified by this study is depicted in Figure 7.2. In short, while economic development policies have contributed to the concentration in jobs in employment subcenters toward the center, west, and northwest of the MCMZ, housing policies have pulled a considerable share of workers further into Eastern-MCMZ. While these trends are consistently increasing the physical separation between jobs and workers (see Chapters 4 and 5), the commodification and fragmentation of public transport systems are increasing transportation costs for workers (see Chapter 6).

The imports substitution policy of the 1940s and the subsequent industrialization of Mexico City locked in the spatial concentration of jobs into its current patterns. The jobs created between the 1940s and 1960s attracted an important number of workers from across the country to Mexico City, who eventually relocated into Eastern-MCMZ. Facing an increasing demand for housing by workers, in the early 1970s the Mexican government instituted state-led housing programs such as the National Workers' Housing Fund (INFONAVIT). While programs like INFONAVIT contributed for a short period to bring workers closer to jobs, the physical separation between jobs and workers saw a new push during the 1990s and the 2000s. In the early 1990s, the INFONAVIT program was reformed into a bank-like system with the goal of advancing housing production through financing private developers and providing soft credits to workers.

The INFONAVIT reform of the 1990s overlapped with a local policy implemented from 2000 to 2005 by the Mexico City government called Bando 2.

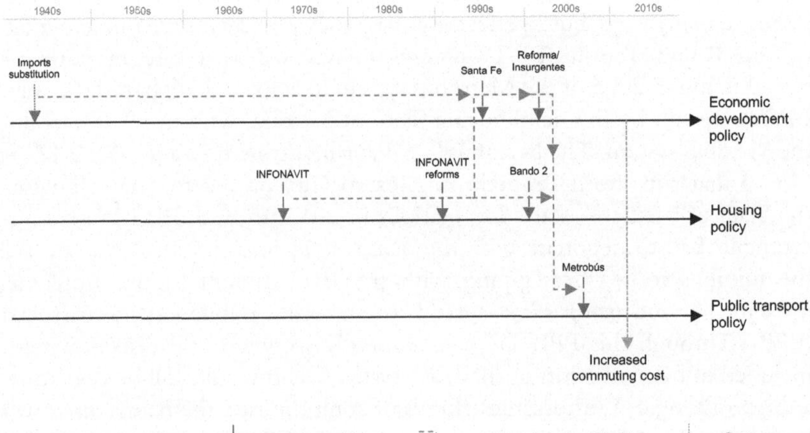

Figure 7.2 Policy interaction II

Through Bando 2, the local government restricted the construction of new housing stock to the four central delegations of the city: Miguel Hidalgo, Cuauhtémoc, Venustiano Carranza, and Benito Juárez. Building social housing in any other of the 12 Mexico City delegations was forbidden by the Bando 2 policy. As the four central delegations had some of the highest land values in the city, the Bando 2 made the construction of social housing for workers in Mexico City financially unfeasible. Administrators of federal housing programs such as INFONAVIT and private developers of social housing navigated these restrictions by moving the construction of social housing for workers into peripheral areas of the MCMZ in the neighboring State of Mexico. The municipalities of the State of Mexico had several characteristics that made them suitable for the development of social housing for workers: commonly owned land hitherto used for agriculture was available for housing development, the price of land was affordable, and the municipalities were willing to grant the construction permits. In short, the coupling of federal housing programs such as INFONAVIT and Bando 2 sparked a process of expansion of social housing for workers into peripheral areas of the MCMZ.

Simultaneously, other kinds of policies contributed to the concentration of jobs in central areas of the urban region and further away from Eastern-MCMZ. Two economic development policies are a case in point. The first is the state-led transformation of a former landfill into a business district in Santa Fe, in the west of Mexico City. As shown in Chapter 4, Santa Fe increased its relevance in the urban structure by moving up from the eleventh to the second most important employment subcenter in the metropolitan region between 1999 and 2019. The second is the reconfiguration of *Paseo de la Reforma* as a service economy global hub during the 1990s. While such state-led redevelopment projects served the purpose of connecting Mexico City to the global centers of finance, service, and management, they also contributed to keep concentrating employment further away from Eastern-MCMZ.

As explained in Chapter 5, there are three salient mechanisms through which the interactions between economic development and housing policies have contributed to shape inequalities in the mobility experience of workers in Eastern-MCMZ. First, workers who arrived at Eastern-MCMZ throughout housing forms of production related to the use value of housing but keep their jobs in existing employment subcenters. By keeping the location of their jobs unchanged, the commuting costs for these workers are increased. Second, workers with formal jobs usually located in employment subcenters who arrived at Eastern-MCMZ through the national housing policy. By using their housing benefits to acquire ownership of a housing unit and moving into peripheral areas, these workers increase their commuting costs overnight. Third, the younger population already residing in Eastern-MCMZ who, by virtue of achieving higher educational attainment win increased access to better, but more distant, primary labor markets. The best jobs in primary labor markets are usually located in employment subcenters, so the Eastern-MCMZ workers who gain access to these labor markets must pay the price of a more costly mobility experience.

The choiceless mobility hypothesis

The application of the PIF to the study of the mobility experience of workers in MCMZ and the empirical evidence presented in Chapters 3 to 6 allows to propose what I call the *choiceless mobility hypothesis* (CMH). I define the CMH as the process through which the interaction between policies from distinct policy domains produce mobility situations that consistently increase the transportation costs for workers. In what follows, I present the defining characteristics of the CMH and situate it within other influential concepts in the literature.

Defining characteristics of the choiceless mobility hypothesis

At its core, the CMH is intended to depict a *process*, not an *outcome*. As the empirical evidence produced by this book demonstrates, the Eastern-MCMZ has some of the highest transportation costs of the metropolitan region (see Chapter 3). The CMH is intended to describe the process through which such an outcome was produced in the first place. Based on the empirical findings presented in Chapters 3 to 6, and on the policy interactions described earlier, I propose the following defining characteristics of the CMH, which are also summarized in Figure 7.3:

1 Urban regions can experience a long-term process of spatial structuring in which the interaction between (i) the spatial location patterns in the demand for labor, (ii) the housing pathways available for workers, and (iii) the political economy of public transport operates to produce geographies of low accessibility to jobs.
2 The interaction between the concentration of jobs in specific employment subcenters and the production of housing for workers in peripheral areas increases workers' mobility needs. Amid a landscape of commodification and fragmentation of public transport systems, the increasing mobility needs of workers increase their transportation costs. Such transportation

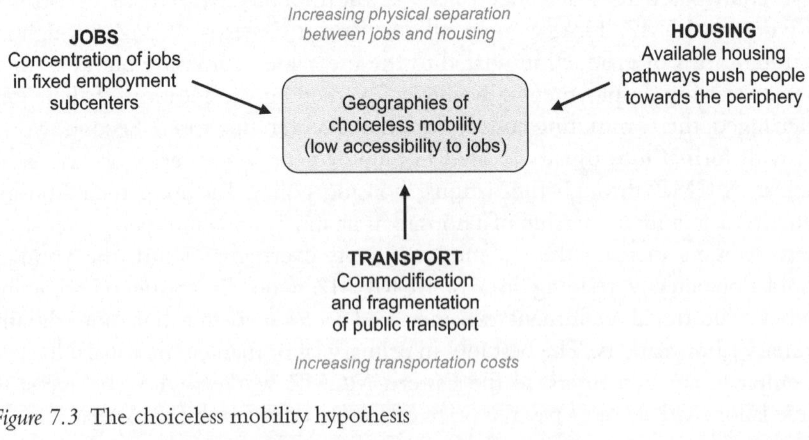

Figure 7.3 The choiceless mobility hypothesis

costs can manifest in an increase of the time and distance that workers allocate to their commute.

3 Workers do not just *choose* to live in low-accessibility territories. Instead, they have no option but to live in such territories due to the lack of alternatives and default housing pathways. The CMH occurs when the economic activities in which workers participate is consistently concentrating in space, while the default housing pathways that are available for them keep increasing both the physical separation between jobs and workers and transportation costs.

Situating the choiceless mobility hypothesis

The literature on mobility and accessibility has developed an array of concepts useful for the analysis of workers' mobility. Available literature includes concepts such as the spatial mismatch hypothesis (Gobillon et al., 2007; Ihlanfeldt & Sjoquist, 1998; Kain, 1968), transport poverty (Lucas, 2012), transport disadvantage (Murray & Davis, 2001), social exclusion (Church et al., 2000; Kenyon, 2003), the limited mobility hypothesis (Calonge, 2018; Faiz, 2011; Lazo & Calderón, 2014), the right to mobility (Cresswell, 2006), transport justice (Martens, 2012, 2017), and mobility justice (Sheller, 2018a, 2018b), among others.[2]

However, the CMH is distinct from these concepts for five reasons. First, most of the previously mentioned concepts were developed within narrow areas of expertise that study either in the geographies of jobs, housing, or transportation. Moving away from the silos approach, the CMH has been developed by examining the interactions between jobs, housing, and transportation. Second, while most of the available concepts are intended to depict an *outcome*, for example, identifying geographies of low accessibility, the CMH is intended to shed light on a *process* that produced such low accessibility geographies in the first place. Third, the available concepts in the literature are usually concerned with better understanding the consequences of living in low accessibility territories. While this is an important academic endeavor, the CMH is more concerned with theorizing the process through which the geographies of low accessibility were configured. Fourth, most of the available concepts take a functionalist approach to low accessibility territories but fall short to further investigate the policy process producing geographies of low accessibility. In this sense, the CMH sheds light on the politics behind the production of low accessibility geographies. Fifth, while most of the concepts available in the literature have been developed to explain the experience of cities in the global north, the CMH has been developed with knowledge from and aiming to explain the urban experience of cities in the Global South.

The physical separation between jobs and housing

The physical separation between jobs and housing has for long occupied a special place in the literature. There is a scholarly tradition researching the spatial mismatch phenomenon within cities. That is, the geographic separation of workers and jobs and its negative consequences for low-income households and disadvantaged minorities (Kain, 1968, 1992; Ihlanfeldt & Sjoquist, 1998; Houston, 2005; Gobillon, Selod, & Zenou, 2007; Hu & Giuliano, 2017; Jin & Paulsen, 2018). Put forward in Kain's (1968) groundbreaking paper, the *spatial mismatch hypothesis* holds that the population that resides in territories with a more balanced households-to-jobs ratio are more likely to find a job and therefore to move forward in the social ladder (Gobillon et al., 2007). The spatial mismatch hypothesis literature has put special attention to the relationship between job/housing balance and mobility at least in two ways. A first body of literature discusses the role of transport infrastructures and transportation modes in the determination of labor market outcomes (Blumenberg et al., 2015; Hu, 2017; Ong & Miller, 2005). A second body discusses the extent to which job accessibility reduces commuting distances and which groups of the population benefit from such proximity (Hu, 2017; Hu & Giuliano, 2017; Levinson, 1998).

The spatial mismatch hypothesis and the CMH are similar in that they both examine the increased physical separation between jobs and housing. However, the two hypotheses are distinct in two fundamental ways. First, while the spatial mismatch hypothesis is concerned with examining the effects of jobs/housing mismatches for labor market outcomes, the CMH is concerned with examining the process through which such physical separation came to be in the first place. That is, while the spatial mismatch hypothesis examines an *outcome*, the CMH examines a *process*. Second, the CMH brings knowledge and nuances from the Global South into the causal explanations put forward by the spatial mismatch hypothesis. This need was first pointed out by Cervero (2013), who argued the spatial mismatch hypothesis, as developed to explain the case of the United States, might unravel in distinct ways in cities of the Global South. This is so because Latin American cities have not urbanized through the same path as the United States cities, and therefore the causal mechanisms of the spatial mismatch hypothesis cannot be applied verbatim to explain the Latin American urban experience.

Transport-related social exclusion

The concept of *transport disadvantage* was developed by Murray and Davis (2001) to refer to the situation in which the people in need of public transit services do not have sufficient public transit service opportunities. This is relevant because transport disadvantage can lead to social disadvantage. By *social disadvantage*, Currie and Delbosc (2010) referred to individuals who either are low-income, are unemployed, or have low political engagement, participation, and social support. Lucas (2012) has pointed out that transport disadvantage and social disadvantage are not necessarily synonyms. Research conducted by Currie and Delbosc (2010) showed that "it is possible to be socially excluded but still have good access to transport or to be transport disadvantaged but highly socially included" (Lucas, 2012: p. 106). Rather, transit disadvantage and social disadvantage can interact to produce what Lucas (2012) called *transit poverty*, "which in turn exacerbates the problems of (in)accessibility to opportunities, services and interactions that increase the risk of becoming socially excluded" (Oviedo & Titheridge, 2016: p. 153). Transport-related social exclusion has been defined by Kenyon et al. (2002) as "the process by which people are prevented from participating in the economic, political and social life of the community because of reduced accessibility to opportunities" (p. 210).

The works by Murray and Davis (2001), Kenyon et al. (2002), Kenyon (2003) and Lucas (2012) have inspired mobility scholars to theorize the *limited mobility hypothesis* (Calonge, 2018; Faiz, 2011; Lazo & Calderón, 2014). This hypothesis is put forward because of transit-related social exclusion and as a strategy used by individuals to cope with such exclusion. According to the limited mobility hypothesis, transit-related social exclusions force the poorest segments of the urban population to limit their search of urban resources to the territories that are most proximate to them. For example, it is argued that urban poor restrict their travel to essential trips related to work, education, and shopping, who "are often confined to walking or at most bicycling, as the weather and topography permits" (Faiz, 2011: p. 40). The limited mobility hypothesis is supported by evidence from studies in cities like Santiago, in Chile (Lazo & Calderón, 2014) and Guadalajara, in México (Calonge, 2018).

The CMH, however, is different from transport-related social exclusion and the limited mobility hypothesis because the workers experiencing the CMH can be both socially included and transport disadvantaged. In this sense, workers in the CMH approach better the circumstance depicted by Lucas (2012) and Currie and Delbosc (2010) in which it is possible to be transport disadvantaged but highly socially included. Indeed, it is precisely access to the jobs located in employment subcenters that increases the transportation costs for workers residing in Eastern-MCMZ. As opposed to the limited mobility hypothesis in which the urban poor restrict their travel to the job locations most proximate to them, in the CMH, workers have no other choice but to commute long distances to reach the employment subcenters while being transport disadvantaged.

The CMH and emerging concepts in the literature

One of the most influential concepts in urban studies literature over the last 20 years is the concept of *accessibility* (Geurs & van Wee, 2004; Levine et al., 2019). This concept was thoroughly discussed in Chapter 2, so it will not be reviewed in-depth again here. Suffice it to say that accessibility assesses the degree to which people can access the resources that cities offer to them by looking at the interactions between land-use patterns (proximity), transportation systems (mobility), and the individual characteristics of urban dwellers (connectivity). There is an intense push to move urban policy analysis from mobility to accessibility (Levine et al., 2019; Martens, 2012; van Wee & Geurs, 2011). Scholars in this effort argue in favor of the instrumental value of mobility as opposed to its intrinsic value. That is, to these scholars, urban dwellers do not move for the sake of movement. Instead, inhabitants move because they want to reach the places that offer urban resources, such as jobs, schools, government services, consumption centers, etc. Accessibility takes the central stage and becomes the main urban attribute to look at from a distributional lens. Mobility becomes a *means* toward the *end* of having increased accessibility. The CMH builds on and is a contribution to the literature on accessibility because it provides analytical lenses to study how accessibility outcomes are produced in the first place.

There are other emerging concepts in the literature such as the right to mobility (Cresswell, 2006), transport justice (Martens, 2012, 2017), and mobility justice (Sheller, 2018a, 2018b). The right to mobility advocates for an understating of mobility as a right tied to notions of citizenship (Cresswell, 2006). Defined as

> the right to move in the urban space, to access places and opportunities, but also the right to stay still . . ., the right to mobility subsumes also the right to accessibility, as fundamentally linked to questions of just access to resources and assets.
>
> (Verlinghieri & Venturini, 2018: p. 127)

The concept of transport justice was put forward by Martens (2012, 2017) as a theoretical basis for a distributional approach to transport. The approach argues that the transport good, defined as accessibility, should be distributed through its own sphere of justice. Martens (2012, 2017) opens up a debate about the distributive principles that should guide transport redistributions. The concept of mobility justice was recently put forward by Sheller (2018a, 2018b) for a debate about the politics behind the production of uneven mobilities—that is, diverging mobility pathways that connect some places while disconnecting others. By asking questions such as *who* is able to exercise the right to mobility and *why*, or *what* governs mobility systems, Sheller (2018a, 2018b) builds a theoretical framework for the analysis of uneven mobility through the lenses of justice.

The difference between the CMH and concepts such as the right to mobility, transport justice, and mobility justice, is one of analytical scope. As described in Chapter 2, the analytical lenses crafted for this study look at the interactions between policies from distinct policy domains in the production of accessibility outcomes. The concepts of right to mobility, transport justice, and mobility justice are narrowly focused on mobility and transport. While useful, these concepts fall short to fully grasp the complexities behind the spatial location of jobs and workers' residential location, which ultimately, I argue, shape the mobility experience of workers. This is where the CMH departs from these emerging concepts and seeks a broader examination of the underlying forces that shape shifts in the urban structure and the population's mobility needs.

Policy implications of the CMH

As discussed earlier, I defined the CMH as a process through which the interaction between policies from distinct policy domains produce mobility situations that consistently increase the transportation costs for workers. As shown through the empirical evidence of Chapters 3 to 6, MCMZ is undergoing a process through which the Eastern-MCMZ is being configured as a geography of low accessibility that consistently increases workers' transportation costs. There are four implications for urban policy analysis derived from the findings of this study.

First, this book shows that the mobility experience of workers is shaped, at least, by the interactions of three policy domains that often work at cross-purposes: economic development, housing, and transport policy. In urban policy practice, it is intuitive to think that the challenges related to the mobility experience should be addressed through transport policy. Nevertheless, as the evidence presented in this book shows, trying to improve the mobility experience resorting exclusively on transport policies will be inevitably misleading and insufficient. However well intentioned, transport policies by themselves will fall short of fully grasping the interaction of transport with economic geographies and default housing pathways. There are approaches in the literature trying to integrate transport and land-use patterns, such as the Transport Oriented Development (TOD) approach (Carlton, 2019; Jamme et al., 2019). However, TOD approaches are limited in that they center their attention in the land-use potential of transport projects in specific places. This approach is closer to frameworks originated within the fields of new urbanism (Talen, 2006, 2020) or smart growth (MacLeod, 2013; Reeds, 2011), than in a comprehensive urban region-scale Policy Interactions Framework. A comprehensive urban policy approach to reduce inequalities in the mobility experience of workers will necessarily need a policy mix with tools from distinct policy domains.

Second, particular attention must be placed on identifying the actors that participate in the policy subsystem of each policy domain and characterizing their specific interests in the policy process. As done in this study, this can be achieved by incorporating the lens of urban political economy into policy analysis. Actors, interests, and strategies to advance their preferred policy solutions must be identified and brought into the analysis. As this book has demonstrated, the outcomes of specific actors' interests within each policy domain can loop back and become an input into the policy process of a different policy silo. This book provides analytical lens to identify such policy feedback effects and incorporate them into urban policy analysis.

Third, we need to find feasible urban policies able to slow down the rate at which geographies of low accessibility are being produced, as well as help the situation of the population currently living under the CMH. One of the main findings of this book is that workers do not just choose to locate in geographies of low accessibility. Instead, they do so because they have no other feasible alternatives due to the default housing pathways. It is in this insight that we might find a way forward to slow down the pace at which geographies of choiceless mobility are being produced: we need to create *alternatives* for workers. This means creating feasible options in several interacting fronts. Alternatives for the spatial location of jobs. Alternatives for the housing pathways available to workers. Alternatives in the ways in which the population commutes to work.

Finally, reducing commuting inequalities needs policy interactions thinking. There is extensive literature about the policy instruments able to produce new employment subcenters. Changes in land-use regulation and productive infrastructure investment are at the forefront of such policy instruments. In terms of housing policy, the need for change is urgent. We need to find housing policies able to bring workers and the low-income population closer to existing employment subcenters. As per public transport policy, there is an urgent need to find policy instruments able to increase the provision of public transport systems as a public and common good. Public transport needs to be de-commodified. The potential of policies such as fares subsidies, public–private partnerships, and direct provision must be explored. But most importantly, scholars, partitioners, and policymakers must start thinking of the mobility experience of workers as a complex urban phenomenon that depends on the interaction of multiple policy domains. Inequalities in mobility experience will not be solved with mobility-, housing-, or economic development-related policies alone. The problem is far too complex to leave it to any one of these policy domains. A policy interactions approach is needed.

Notes

1 For a detailed explanation of the Policy Interactions Framework, see Chapter 2.
2 For a thorough review of these concepts, refer to Chapter 2.

References

Blumenberg, E., Pierce, G., & Smart, M. (2015). Transportation access, residential location, and economic opportunity: Evidence from two housing voucher experiments. *Cityscape: A Journal of Policy Development and Research*, *17*(2), 89–111.

Calonge, F. (2018). Recursos de movilidad y accesibilidad urbana en los municipios del sur del Área Metropolitana de Guadalajara, México. *Revista Urbano*, *38*, 48–57.

Carlton, I. (2019). Transit planners' transit-oriented development-related practices and theories. *Journal of Planning Education and Research*, *39*(4), 508–519.

Cervero, R. (2013). Linking urban transport and land use in developing countries. *Journal of Transport and Land Use*, *6*(1), 7–24.

Church, A., Frost, M., & Sullivan, K. (2000). Transport and social exclusion in London. *Transport Policy*, 7, 195–205.

Cresswell, T. (2006). The right to mobility: The production of mobility in the courtroom. *Antipode*, *38*(4), 735–754.

Currie, G., & Delbosc, A. (2010). Modelling the social and psychological impacts of transport disadvantage. *Transportation*, *37*(6), 953–966.

Faiz, A. (2011). Transportation and the urban poor. *ITE Journal (Institute of Transportation Engineers), 81*(12), 40–43.

Geurs, K. T., & van Wee, B. (2004). Accessibility evaluation of land-use and transport strategies: Review and research directions. *Journal of Transport Geography, 12*(2), 127–140.

Gobillon, L., Selod, H., & Zenou, Y. (2007). The mechanisms of spatial mismatch. *Urban Studies, 44*(12), 2401–2428.

Houston, D. S. (2005). Methods to test the spatial mismatch hypothesis. *Economic Geography, 81*(4), 407–434.

Hu, L. (2017). Job accessibility and employment outcomes: Which income groups benefit the most? *Transportation, 44*(6), 1421–1443.

Hu, L., & Giuliano, G. (2017). Poverty concentration, job access, and employment outcomes. *Journal of Urban Affairs, 39*(1), 1–16.

Ihlanfeldt, K. R., & Sjoquist, D. L. (1998). The spatial mismatch hypothesis: A review of recent studies and their implications for welfare reform. *Housing Policy Debate, 9*(4), 849–892.

Jamme, H. T., Rodriguez, J., Bahl, D., & Banerjee, T. (2019). A twenty-five-year biography of the TOD concept: From design to policy, planning, and implementation. *Journal of Planning Education and Research, 39*(4), 409–428.

Jin, J., & Paulsen, K. (2018). Does accessibility matter? Understanding the effect of job accessibility on labour market outcomes. *Urban Studies, 55*(1), 91–115.

Kain, J. F. (1968). Housing segregation, negro employment, and metropolitan decentralization. *The Quarterly Journal of Economics, 82*(2), 175–197.

Kain, J. F. (1992). The spatial mismatch hypothesis: Three decades later. *Housing Policy Debate, 3*(2), 371–460.

Kenyon, S. (2003). Understanding social exclusion and social inclusion. *Municipal Engineer, 156*(ME2), 97–104.

Kenyon, S., Lyons, G., & Rafferty, J. (2002). Transport and social exclusion: Investigating the possibility of promoting inclusion through virtual mobility. *Journal of Transport Geography, 10*, 207–219.

Lazo, A., & Calderón, R. (2014). Los anclajes en la proximidad y la movilidad cotidiana. Retrato de tres barrios de la ciudad de Santiago de Chile. *Eure, 40*(121), 207–226.

Levine, J., Grengs, J., & Merlin, L. A. (2019). *From mobility to accessibility: Transforming urban transportation and land-use planning*. Ithaca: Cornell University Press.

Levinson, D. M. (1998). Accessibility and the journey to work. *Journal of Transport Geography, 6*(1), 11–21.

Lucas, K. (2012). Transport and social exclusion: Where are we now? *Transport Policy, 20*, 105–113.

MacLeod, G. (2013). New urbanism/smart growth in the Scottish highlands: Mobile policies and post-politics in local development planning. *Urban Studies, 50*(11), 2196–2221.

Martens, K. (2012). Justice in transport as justice in accessibility: Applying Walzer's "Spheres of Justice" to the transport sector. *Transportation, 39*(6), 1035–1053.

Martens, K. (2017). *Transport justice*. New York and London: Routledge.

Murray, A. T., & Davis, R. (2001). Equity in regional service provision. *Journal of Regional Science, 41*(4), 577–600.

Ong, P., & Miller, D. (2005). Spatial and transportation mismatch in Los Angeles. *Journal of Planning Education and Research, 25*, 43–56.

Oviedo, D., & Titheridge, H. (2016). Mobilities of the periphery: Informality, access and social exclusion in the urban fringe in Colombia. *Journal of Transport Geography, 55*, 152–164.

Reeds, J. (2011). *Smart growth: From sprawl to sustainability*. Cambridge: Green Books.

Sheller, M. (2018a). *Mobility justice: The politics of movement in an age of extremes*. New York: Verso.

Sheller, M. (2018b). Theorising mobility justice. *Tempo Social, 30*(2), 17–34.

Talen, E. (2006). Connecting new urbanism and American planning: An historical interpretation. *Urban Design International, 11*(2), 83–98.

Talen, E. (2020). *A research agenda for New Urbanism*. Cheltenham and Northampton: Edward Elgar Publishing.

van Wee, B., & Geurs, K. T. (2011). Discussing equity and social exclusion in accessibility evaluations. *European Journal of Transport and Infrastructure Research, 11*(4), 350–367.

Verlinghieri, E., & Venturini, F. (2018). Exploring the right to mobility through the 2013 mobilizations in Rio de Janeiro. *Journal of Transport Geography, 67*, 126–136.

Annex

Employment subcenters in Mexico City Metropolitan Zone, 1999 and 2019

Subcenters in 1999 (Agebs):

1. Central Agglomeration

0901500010790	0901500010945	0901000010991	0901500010979	0901400010346
0901600010590	0901500010998	0901500010822	0901600010641	0901400010613
0901500010818	0901600010779	0901000011006	0901500010589	0901600010393
0901500010930	0901500011089	0901500010983	0901500010659	0901500011233
0901500010729	0901500011341	0901000010987	0901400010543	0901500011055
090160001050A	0901500010663	0901400010929	0901400010350	0901600010656
0901500010803	0901500011093	0901500010911	0901400010825	0901400010859
0901400010098	0901500010860	0901400010952	0901500010644	090160001118A
0901400010223	0901500011360	0901400010914	0901400010399	0901000011241
0901600011211	0901600010459	090150001106A	0901500011036	0901600010054
0901500010964	0901500011214	0901400010755	090140001069A	0901000010135
0901500010837	0901600010482	0901600010711	0901600011029	0901500010466
0901500010767	0901400010045	0901500011110	0901600010637	0901400010632
090150001049A	0901500010894	0901600011194	0901600011207	0901400011005
0901600010571	0901600010675	0901500011411	0901400010793	0901400010261
090150001095A	0901500011430	090160001075A	0901400010257	0901400010774
0901600010622	0901700011045	0901400010384	0901600010891	0901500010485
0901700010687	0901500010752	0901500010856	0901600010463	0901400010079
0901600010834	0901000011133	0901500011106	0901600010285	0901400010187
0901500010875	0901500010786	0901500010926	0901400010609	0901000011044
090160001068A	0901500011182	0901400010721	0901600010783	0901600010995
0901600010849	0901000011059	0901600011175	0901000011203	0901000011129
0901600011226	0901400010844	0901500011040	0901400010064	0901000011237
0901500011445	0901500010748	0901400010562	0901500011125	0901600011156
0901500011356	0901500011017	0901400010558	0901600010177	0901400010740
0901400010204	0901600010694	0901600010730	0901400010971	0901500010733
0901400010242	0901400010365	0901600010707	0901000010972	0901600010444
090150001070A	0901400010219	090140001083A	090150001113A	0901500011197
0901500010907	0901500010697	090140001005A	0901600011160	0901500010841
0901600010660	090150001088A	0901500011002	0901400010401	0901500010998
0901600010478	0901400010238	0901500010536	0901400010736	0901600010779
0901400010100	0901500010682	0901500011163	0901600010158	

0901500010771 0901400010806 0901400010191 0901400010420
0901400010933 090150001145A 0901400010702 0901400010416
0901400010717 0901600010603 0901500011074 090100001110A
090150001120A 0901400010577 0901400010990 0901500010678
0901500010945 0901500010714 0901400010810 0901400010628

2. Naucalpan
150570001018A 1505700011474 0901600010092 1505700011559 150570001153A
1505700011440 1505700011489 1505700010353 150570001146A
150570001139A 1505700010368 1505700011544 1505700011510

3. Tlalnepantla
151040001029A 1510400011885 1510400010406 1510400011936
1510400011809 151040001189A 1510400010302 1510400011940 1510400010976
1510400011870 1510400010393 1510400010410 1510400010961

4. Mercado de Abastos
0900700014895 0900700012403 0900700010750 0900700013651 0900700013666
0900700012390 0900700012475

5. Iztacalco 1
0900600010274 0900600010293 0900600010132 0900600011094 0900600011107

6. Azcapotzalco 1
0900200010877 0900200010881

7. Ecatepec
1503300010667 150330001078A 1503300010987 1503300011059 1503300011114
1503300013534 1503300010845 150330001103A

8. Cuautitlán 1
1512100010252 1512100010267 1512100010303 1512100010356

9. Perisur
090100001128A 0901000011307 0900300011105 0901200011956

10. Acapotzalco/Cuauhtémoc
0901500010057 090150001017A 0901500010042 0900200010769

11. Santa Fe
0900400010195 0901000011379 0901000011542

12. Azcapotzalco 2
0900200011023 0900200010665 0900200010650

13. Coyoacán
0900300010075 0900300010164 090030001015A

14. Iztacalco 2
0900600010185 0900600010310

15. Gustavo A. Madero 1
0900500011646 0900500011627

16. Iztapalapa 2
0900700011180 0900700011176

17. Xochimilco
0901300010014 0901300010067

18. Tepotzotlán
1509500010195 1509500010208

19. Cuautitlán 2
1512100010093 1512100010106

20. Álvaro Obregón
0901000010116 0901000011805

21. Gustavo A. Madero 2
0900500011256 0900500011400

22. Tlalpan
0901200011918 0901200010233

Subcenters in 2019 (Agebs):

1. Central Agglomeration

0901500010589	0901500011089	0901600010783	0901600011029	0901400010933
0901500010659	0901500011182	0901600010656	0901600010891	0901400010914
0901500010644	0901500011110	0901600010641	090140001005A	0901000010972
0901500010536	0901500011106	0901600010779	0901400010242	0901000010987
0901500010663	0901500011214	090160001075A	0901400010257	0901000010991
0901500010752	090150001120A	0901600010637	0901400010261	0901000011059
0901500010786	0901500011125	0901600010834	0901400010238	0901000011044
0901500010771	090150001113A	0901600010872	0901400010399	0901000011186
0901500010767	0901500011144	0901600010995	0901400010401	090100001110A
0901500010907	0901500011233	0901500010818	0901400010416	0901000011129
0901500010894	0901500010837	0901500010803	0901400010204	0901000011203
090150001088A	0901500010926	0901500010945	0901400010384	0901000011241
0901500010964	0901500010822	0901500010930	0901400010609	0901000011133
0901500010733	0901500010678	0901500010790	0901400010613	0900300010249
0901500010748	0901500010682	090160001068A	0901400010740	0900300010111
0901500010860	0901500010697	0901600010444	0901400010755	0900300010126
0901500010875	0901600010482	0901600010622	0901400010825	0900300010130
090150001049A	0901600010590	0901600010730	090140001083A	0900300010145
0901500010485	0901600010603	0901600010849	0901400010844	090030001015A
0901500010714	0901600010707	0901500011356	0901400010952	0900300010164
090150001070A	0901600010711	0901500011341	0901400010558	0900300010075
0901500010729	0901600010694	090150001145A	0901400010562	0900300010060
0901500010856	0901600010478	0901500011445	0901400010577	0901600011226
0901500010841	0901600010571	0901500011430	090140001069A	0901400010223
090150001095A	0901600010463	0901500011337	0901400010702	0901400010219
0901500010983	0901600010459	0901500011318	0901400010793	0901400010717
0901500011017	0901600010552	0901500011411	0901400010736	
0901500011002	0901600010340	090160001118A	0901400010806	
0901500010998	0901600010675	0901600011175	0901400010810	
0901500011093	0901600010660	0901600011160	0901400010929	

2. Santa Fe

0900400010195	0900400010104	0901000011379	0901000012358	0901000011472
0900400010354	0900400010369	0901000011542		

3. Naucalpan

1505700010122	150570001139A	1505700011489	150570001146A	1505700011559
150570001018A	1505700011351	1505700010368	150570001153A	1505700010353
1505700011328	1505700011474	1505700011455	1505700011544	0901600010092
1505700011385				

4. Tlalnepantla
1510400011809 151040001189A 1510400010302 1510400011940 1505700011192
151040001029A 1510400010393 1510400010410 1510400010976 1505700010048
1510400011870 1510400010406 1510400011936 1510400010961 150570001121A
1510400011885 1510400010251

5. Mercado de Abastos
0900700012390 0900700010750 0900700013651 0900700012475 0900700014895
0900700012403

6. Perisur
0900800010086 0900800010283 090100001128A 0901200012070 0901200010074
0900800010194 0901000011260 0901000011307 0901200011956 0900300011105

7. Azcapotzalco 1
0900200011165 0900200010877 0900200010881 0900500010883

8. Aeropuerto
0901700010140 0901700010475

9. Cuautitlán 1
1512100010252 1512100010267 1512100010303 1502400010051

10. Benito Juárez/Obregón
0901400010187 0901400010350 0901400010346 0901000010135 0901000010421

11. Ecatepec 1
1503300010667 1503300013534 150330001078A 1503300010845 1503300010987

12. Miguel Hidalgo 1
0901600011264 0901600011245

13. Cuautitlán 2
1512100010106 1512100010093 1512100010144 151210001013A

14. Iztacalco
0900600010293 0900600010132 0900600011094

15. Ecatepec 2
1503300014886 150330001046A

16. Tultitlán 1
1510900031769 1510900030614

17. Acapotzalco/Cuauhtémoc
0900200010769 0901500010042 090150001017A 0901500010057

18. Huixquilucan/Cuajimalpa
1503700710098 1503700710100

19. Ecatepec 3
1503300011059 1503300011114

20. Miguel Hidalgo 2
0901600010425 0901600010410 0901600010514

21. Tepotzotlán
1509500010195 1509500010208 1509500010161

22. Tultitlán 2
1510900010347 1510900010351

23. Iztapalapa 2
0900700011176 0900700011180

24. Iztapalapa 3
0900700014698 0900700015198

25. Texcoco
1509900010796 1509900011309 1509900010828

26. Tlalpan
0901200010182 0901200010411 0901200010430

27. Cuauhtémoc/Juárez
0901500011498 0901400010030

28. Chalco
1502500011235 1502500010129

29. Gustavo A. Madero
0900500011627 0900500011646

Postscript: researching the mobility experience of workers amid the COVID-19 pandemic

This book was written amid the COVID-19 pandemic. As I write this postscript in March 2022, the COVID-19 public health emergency is still an ongoing global event. While this book does not discuss the implications of the global pandemic for the mobility experience of workers, the results of this study will remain relevant for urban policy research in a post-pandemic world. The purpose of this postscript is to propose new avenues for urban research around policy interactions and the mobility experience of workers that have been opened by the ongoing COVID-19 pandemic.

Policy interactions derived from the pandemic response

Governments throughout the world and from all branches and levels rushed to implement policies designed to curb COVID-19 infection rates. Such policies will inevitably overlap in urban space and interact with pre-pandemic existing public policies. The foreseeable outcomes of such policy interactions remain unknown and understudied. For example, the long-standing tradition in Mexican cities of providing public transit through a concessions system, in which public transport is privately owned and managed, is interacting with remote working policies, non-essential business closures, and health-related measures in transport management.[1] The COVID-19-related measures caused a drastic drop in public transport ridership across Mexican cities. As there is virtually no subsidy from the government for the operation of bus concessioners, the sole source of revenue for privately owned public transport is the fee paid by users. The drop in ridership produced a dramatic drop in revenue, jeopardizing the financial sustainability of the concessions system. This example raises some questions. Is the concessions system the most appropriate scheme to overcome shocks such as those produced by the COVID-19 pandemic? What kind of institutional change is needed to prepare public transport in Mexican cities for whatever the next shock is? Has the pandemic created a window of opportunity to advance reform in the public transport system aiming to provide transport as a public or a common good? This is only one example of the kind of research about policy interactions derived from the pandemic response. More policy interactions should be explored.

Accessibility without moving

The literature on urban accessibility is based on the following premise: cities offer urban resources to its inhabitants, and such resources are distributed across urban space. If urban dwellers wish to access such resources, they must move to reach the places offering them. Nevertheless, the global pandemic showed us that there can be circumstances in which the urban population will not be able to move, like in mandatory lockdowns. Such circumstances can be prolonged by months. This raises the question of accessibility without moving. As we saw during the pandemic, some sectors of the population were able to keep accessing key urban resources like their jobs, receiving groceries, remote schooling, and so forth. People with white-collar jobs in sectors like finance, education, the knowledge economy, and the like had no trouble performing their jobs from home and kept receiving a paycheck. However, other sectors of the population saw their access to urban resources interrupted by the lockdown. Workers in face-to-face industries such as manufacturing or some types of jobs in the service economy could simply not perform remotely. In the absence of a robust social safety net, like in the case of most countries in the Global South, these workers had to decide between not receiving an income or going out to work amid the pandemic, thus putting their health and lives at risk. This example applies to many other urban resources distributed across urban space ranging from consumer goods to broadband Internet, to quality public space, hospitals, and so forth.

In short, we have the challenge of designing urban policies to secure the population's accessibility to urban resources without moving. The ongoing pandemic can provide us with invaluable research settings to assess the factors enabling and obstructing accessibility without moving. This once-in-a-hundred years research-setting opportunity must be seized. In this occasion, we faced a global pandemic. But tomorrow, we might face a natural disaster or any other kind of emergency that would make us immobile once again.

Accelerated transition toward remote work

The global pandemic accelerated a long-standing trend of transitioning toward remote work. Today, many companies in high value-added industries are exploring the possibility of continuing with remote work even after the pandemic ends. Influential urban scholars are discussing whether urban agglomerations will continue to be an important productive force after the pandemic.[2] This raises important questions for urban research. What are the implications for urban labor markets of this accelerated transition to remote work in urban regions? What about the implications for urban land markets? How will the transition toward remote work affect urban form and the mobility experience of workers? Which industries will succeed in transitioning toward remote work, which will not, and why? How would an accelerated transition toward remote work affect public transport policy? The pandemic has provided us with the possibility to conduct empirical investigation about the possible consequences of a remote work transition. Such research can be used for policy development.

The future of social safety nets

The elephant in the room is existing social safety nets in the Global South. As the empirical chapters in this book have shown, even before the pandemic, workers in Mexico City Metropolitan Zone lived with very limited spatial options both in terms of jobs and housing. When the pandemic hit, the perils of workers were exacerbated. In facing the pandemic, one would have expected that the government provided a robust safety net for vulnerable workers, especially those in the informal economy. There was virtually no safety net to protect workers during their pandemic downfall. Laid-off workers had no unemployment insurance to resort to. School closings put the weight of childcare on the shoulders of workers, forcing many women to abandon the labor force. Workers in the informal economy had no option but to keep going out to work, putting their health and that of their families at risk. The list of hardships faced by workers goes on. The pandemic showed us a new face of the excruciating vulnerability of our social safety net, which raises several research questions. What is the kind of social safety net that would ameliorate hardship in times of economic and sanitary shocks? How do we expand the social safety net not only to protect formal workers but to include workers in the informal economy? What would it take to achieve such structural reform in the social safety net of countries in the Global South? As the famous saying goes, "never let a good crisis go to waste."

Notes

1 *El Universal* (7/19/2020) "Transporte, choferes y usuarios se reparten culpas por COVID." Retrieved on 2/23/2021 from https://tinyurl.com/y73lsh8x.

2 Richard Florida (12/10/2020) "Will Coronavirus Be the Death of Cities? Not So Fast." *The Wall Street Journal*, retrieved on 2/23/2021 from https://tinyurl.com/y7zc8t55; John Rennie Short & Michael J. Orlando (1/25/2021) "Why COVID-19 won't kill cities." *The Conversation*, retrieved on 2/23/2021 from https://tinyurl.com/y5rtm99v; Ian Goldin & Robert Muggah (9/4/2020) "Coronavirus hasn't killed the city. Here's why." World Economic Forum, retrieved on 2/23/2021 from https://tinyurl.com/yb34mx93.

Index

Note: Page numbers in *italics* and **bold** indicate Figures and Tables, respectively.